A Trip Through the NFL Attic
or
The Game You Thought You Knew

Find two or more pro football fans, throw them a question or 100, and chances are good that before long you'll have an argument going on some minor point! The game is like that...full of minutiae that at times can stump even the proudest trivia experts. Here, for the first time, is a collection to test the wits of football fans, no matter what their age or knowledge-ability.

The First Official NFL Trivia Book contains quiz questions, lists of pro football accomplishments, and a mass of data that only *looks* insignificant (the stuff that true trivialists thrive on!) By the way, can *you* name the famous American novelist who got his start as a cub reporter covering the Pottsville Maroons?

Other Sports Books from SIGNET

☐ **INSTANT REPLAY: The Green Bay Diary of Jerry Kramer edited by Dick Schaap.** From the locker room to the goal line, from the training field to the Super Bowl, this is the inside story of a great pro-football team . . . "The best behind the scenes glimpse of pro football ever produced."—*The New York Times* (#E9657—$2.50)

☐ **PAPER LION by George Plimpton.** When a first-string writer suits-up to take his lumps as a last-string quarterback for the Detroit Lions, the result is "the best book ever about pro football!"—*Red Smith.* "A great book that makes football absolutely fascinating to fan and non-fan alike . . . a tale to gladden the envious heart of every weekend athlete."—*The New York Times* (#J7668—$1.95)

☐ **PLAYING PRO FOOTBALL TO WIN by John Unitas, with Harold Rosenthal.** A bruising inside look at the pro game by the greatest quarterback of them all. Revised and updated. (#W7209—$1.50)

☐ **SCREWBALL by Tug McGraw and Joseph Durso.** "You gotta believe!" when baseball's star reliever and super flake rips the cover off the game he plays and life he's led . . . "It's the best!"—Roger Kahn, author of *The Boys of Summer* in *The New York Times* Includes an action-packed photo insert. (#Y6421—$1.25)

☐ **THE PERFECT JUMP by Dick Schaap.** What happens to a world-record-breaking athlete when he's reached that once-in-a-lifetime perfection he can never achieve again? The glory and heartbreak of an athlete who reached the top and had nowhere left to go. With an exciting sports photo insert! (#E7248—$1.75)

THE FIRST OFFICIAL NFL TRIVIA BOOK

BY
TED BROCK
AND
JIM CAMPBELL

A SIGNET BOOK

NEW AMERICAN LIBRARY

TIMES MIRROR

All contents are accurate as of July 1, 1980

Contents

NFL Trivia Quiz

Unless we miss our guess, your chances of a perfect score on the 150 questions that follow are razor-thin. But that's to be expected from an exercise as trivial as this one. You'll notice, along the way, that we've thrown in some random tidbits culled from the NFL's 60-year history. Think of them as "breathers" if you like . . . when you're dealing with microscopic information. it helps to give your eyes a rest, a "freebie" if you will. every now and then. Answers to the quiz begin on page 165.

1. Side by side

Which two NFL running backs played in the same college backfield?

   a. O.J. Simpson and Ricky Bell
   b. Tony Dorsett and Otis Armstrong
   c. Sherman Smith and Earl Campbell
   d. Franco Harris and Lydell Mitchell
   e. Walter Payton and Roland Harper
   f. Rob Lytle and Rob Carpenter

2. Running against the grain

Identify the running back whose number was/is NOT 32:

   a. Jim Brown
   b. Gale Sayers
   c. Franco Harris
   d. O.J. Simpson
   e. Ottis Anderson
   f. Cullen Bryant

3. Also-rans?

O.J. Simpson holds the NFL record for scoring 23 touchdowns in a season. Identify the pair of running backs who are tied for second place with 22.

   a. Larry Brown and Franco Harris
   b. Sam Cunningham and Ricky Bell
   c. Dick Bass and John Cappelletti
   d. Jim Brown and Steve Van Buren
   e. Gale Sayers and Chuck Foreman
   f. Pete Banaszak and Paul Hornung

4. Now batting for WHOM?

Which former 49ers running back was the only man ever to pinch-hit for the legendary Ted Williams?

   a. Hugh McElhenny
   b. Carroll Hardy
   c. Jim Brown
   d. Chuck Essegian
   e. Y.A. Tittle
   f. Vic Janowicz

A curious set of statistics might serve to point out the injection of new life into the passing game around the NFL during recent years. To wit: In 1977, quarterbacks registered five performances of 300 yards or better during the 14-game regular season. In 1978, with a 16-game schedule in effect, there were 11 300-plus performances. In 1979, San Diego's Dan Fouts alone had six outings where he passed for 300 yards or more; the league total in this category was 44. The numbers speak of the prowess of Fouts and his entire offensive unit, to be sure. But consider, too, the adoption of the "single chuck" rule in 1978, limiting a defensive back to one contact with a receiver, and that within a zone five yards beyond the line of scrimmage. And in 1979, NFL officials were instructed to be quicker in whistling a play dead when a quarterback was clearly in the grasp of a tackler.

5. Good stock

Which member of the Atlanta Falcons is the son of a Samoan chieftain?

    a. Rolland Lawrence
    b. Wilson Faumuina
    c. Steve Bartkowski
    d. Garth Ten Napel
    e. Fulton Kuykendall
    f. Bubba Bean

6. Goal-oriented

Who holds the NFL record for scoring in the most consecutive games (151)?

    a. George Blanda
    b. Fred Cox
    c. Gino Cappelletti
    d. Gale Sayers
    e. Walter Payton
    f. Lenny Moore

Rolland Lawrence, the Atlanta Falcons' star cornerback, was an outstanding offensive player at tiny Tabor College in Hillsboro, Kansas. As a running back, Lawrence (5 feet 10 inches, 179 pounds), from Franklin, Pennsylvania, gained over 4,000 yards.

7. Man for two seasons

Who is the only man to manage a major league baseball team and coach an NFL football team?

a. Casey Stengel
b. Charlie Dressen
c. Hugo Bezdek
d. Dan Jesse
e. Frank Leahy
f. Clark Shaughnessy

8. Penetrate this one

Complete the famous front-four combinations.

a. Rams: Lamar Lundy, Rosey Grier, Deacon Jones, and _____.

b. Vikings: Jim Marshall, Gary Larsen, Carl Eller, and _____.

c. Steelers: L.C. Greenwood, Dwight White, Ernie Holmes, and _____.

d. Dolphins: Vern Den Herder, Bob Heinz, Bill Stanfill, and _____.

e. Cowboys: Harvey Martin, Larry Cole, Randy White and _____.

9. Welcome

True or false? The Pro Football Hall of Fame's class of 1980 includes Bob Lilly, Deacon Jones, Jim Otto, and Willie Wood.

10. Precocious

Name the two members of the Pro Football Hall of Fame who played only junior college football before playing in the NFL.

11. The whole enchilada

Which man played more seasons, more games, and scored more points than anyone in NFL history?

    a. Jim Brown
    b. Fran Tarkenton
    c. Jim Marshall
    d. Jim Turner
    e. Johnny Unitas
    f. George Blanda

12. Clockwork

Jim Marshall, the 42-year-old Minnesota Vikings defensive end, retired at the end of the 1979 season with the NFL record for consecutive games played. How many?

    a. 1,230
    b. 150
    c. 282
    d. 521
    e. 88
    f. 310

13. Idles of March

Which NFL player was NOT an outstanding track athlete as well?

   a. Curley Culp
   b. Clifford Branch
   c. Mel Gray
   d. Bob Hayes
   e. O.J. Simpson
   f. Larry Burton

14. Triple threat

Name the man who played halfback in the NFL, umpired major league baseball, and coached professional basketball.

   a. Clarence Peaks
   b. Volney Quinlan
   c. Larry Brown
   d. Hank Soar
   e. Burl Toler
   f. Jim Tunney

Pro Football Hall of Fame member Bobby Layne and three-time All-American Doak Walker played together in the Detroit Lions' backfield for six years in the 1950s. Layne and Walker had played quarterback and halfback together at Highland Park High School in Dallas.

15. Five figures

Only two rushers in NFL history have gained more than 10,000 yards rushing in their careers. Name them.

a. Jim Brown and Jim Taylor
b. Jim Brown and Bill Brown
c. Jim Brown and O.J. Simpson
d. O.J. Simpson and Franco Harris
e. O.J. Simpson and Larry Csonka
f. O.J. Simpson and Don Perkins

16. But can he dunk?

Which NFL wide receiver is a son-in-law of the famous basketball dribbling wizard, Marques Haynes?

a. Mike Haynes, Patriots
b. Drew Pearson, Cowboys
c. Lynn Swann, Steelers
d. Billy Ryckman, Falcons
e. James Lofton, Packers
f. Guido Merkens, Oilers

On a two-game trip to Japan and Hawaii in 1976, the San Diego Chargers got in two workouts in one day. Unusual? Not until you consider that the two sessions were 3,700 miles apart. After training in Tokyo on a Thursday morning, the team caught a 7:30 p.m. flight, crossed the international date line, and reached Honolulu at 6:30 a.m. the same day, just in time for a few hours' sleep and another workout that afternoon.

17. Undergraduate work

Which present-day NFL running back holds the NCAA rushing record with 6,082 yards in a four-year college career?

  a. Archie Griffin, Bengals
  b. Franco Harris, Steelers
  c. Lydell Mitchell, Chargers
  d. Tony Dorsett, Cowboys
  e. Art Best, Bears
  f. Ted McKnight, Chiefs

18. Signed and delivered

Who was the first player chosen in the NFL's first draft in 1936 to actually play in the NFL?

  a. Sammy Baugh
  b. Riley Smith
  c. Don Hutson
  d. Jay Berwanger
  e. Dan Fortmann
  f. Armand Niccolai

19. It exists, he exists

Name the all-pro performer from Ouachita Baptist University.

  a. Cliff Harris, Cowboys
  b. Carlos Pennywell, Patriots
  c. John Stallworth, Steelers
  d. Pat Thomas, Rams
  e. Brad Van Pelt, Giants
  f. Ken Houston, Redskins

20. He had to start somewhere

Which American novelist began his writing career as a cub reporter covering an NFL team—the Pottsville (Pennsylvania) Maroons—in the 1920s?

  a. John O'Hara
  b. Ernest Hemingway
  c. F. Scott Fitzgerald
  d. James Jones
  e. Norman Mailer
  f. John Updike

21. Heady topic

What is unique about the Cleveland Browns' helmet?

  a. The Browns are the only team that still uses leather helmets.
  b. The helmets glow in the dark.
  c. They are equipped with citizens band radios.
  d. They cost $500 each.
  e. The Browns are the only NFL team not displaying a logo.
  f. The Browns are the only NFL team to have "home" and "away" helmets.

22. Airborne

Which NFL receiver teamed with Y.A. Tittle to introduce the "Alley Oop" pass?

a. Frank Gifford
b. R.C. Owens
c. Clyde Connor
d. Bobby Walston
e. Billy Howton
f. Billy Wilson

23. New baby

By what name was the National Football League known during its first two seasons, 1920 and 1921?

a. United Football League
b. American Football League
c. American Professional Football Association
d. National Professional Football League
e. All-America Football Conference
f. Continental Football League

24. Pioneers

The Green Bay Packers' franchise is unique for two reasons. One is that it represents the NFL's smallest city. What is the other?

a. It is the oldest franchise in the league.
b. It is community-owned.
c. It has never won a championship.
d. Its stadium is the only one in the league without lights.
e. It began play as part of the United Football League.
f. All its head coaches have been ex-Packers players.

In the 1965 playoff for the Western Division championship of the NFL, Baltimore's Tom Matte played the entire game at quarterback with the Colts' game plan taped to his wrist. Starter Johnny Unitas and backup Gary Cuozzo both were injured, and Matte, a running back who had played quarterback at Ohio State, got the call—and the NFL's first portable "crib sheet." The Colts lost to Green Bay 13–10 in sudden death overtime.

25. "You can call me ..."

Match the player from the first column with his given name in the second column.

1. Bubba Bean		a.	Mikel
2. Rocky Bleier		b.	David
3. Rusty Chambers		c.	Charles
4. Boobie Clark		d.	Charles
5. Buddy Hardeman		e.	Robert
6. Bo Harris		f.	Clint
7. Ike Harris		g.	Isiah
8. Rusty Jackson		h.	Russell
9. Butch Johnson		i.	Ernst
10. Bo Matthews		j.	Willie
11. Steve Mike-Mayer		k.	Dalton
12. Tinker Owens		l.	Istvan
13. Bo Rather		m.	William

26. Around the clock

Called "The Last of the 60-Minute Men," this Pro Football Hall of Famer played nearly the entire game in a series of crucial victories as his team drove for the 1960 NFL title. Who is he?

a. Chuck Bednarik, Eagles
b. Sam Huff, Giants
c. Bill George, Bears
d. Ray Nitschke, Packers
e. Dave Wilcox, 49ers
f. Joe Schmidt, Lions

The first NFL championship played indoors was not Super Bowl XII in the New Orleans Superdome. It was the 1932 meeting between the Portsmouth Spartans and the Chicago Bears, held at Chicago Stadium, a hockey rink that afforded an 80-yard field covered with dirt left over from a recent circus. The Bears beat the Spartans 9–0, scoring their touchdown on a pass from Bronko Nagurski to Red Grange and later adding a safety.

27. On the rebound

Name the NFL coach who delayed his NFL playing career a year to play one season with the Minneapolis Lakers of the NBA in 1950–51.

   a. Tom Landry, Cowboys
   b. Bud Grant, Vikings
   c. Bill Walsh, 49ers
   d. Pete Gent, Giants
   e. Sam Rutigliano, Browns
   f. Ray Malavasi, Rams

28. Hint: They're not cousins

What do the following have in common?
   Don Horn
   Dennis Shaw
   Brian Sipe
   Bill Donckers
   Jesse Freitas

29. Busy man

Name the pro halfback who gained 1,432 yards rushing and 1,442 yards passing in a single season.

   a. Bobby Douglass, Chicago Bears, 1968
   b. Orban (Spec) Sanders, New York Yankees (AAFC), 1947
   c. Beattie Feathers, Chicago Bears, 1934
   d. Roger Staubach, Dallas Cowboys, 1976
   e. Norm Van Brocklin, Philadelphia Eagles, 1957
   f. Buddy Young, Brooklyn Dodgers (AAFC), 1949

30. Good resume

Although he did not play college football, he was a successful high school head coach, college assistant and head coach, and a pro assistant before being elevated to the head coaching job of the Detroit Lions in the 1970s. Who is he?

    a. Joe Schmidt
    b. Tommy Hudspeth
    c. Rick Forzano
    d. Lou Holtz
    e. Harry Gilmer
    f. Bud Grant

31. He lived for fourth down

Which NFL player holds the record for the most career punts, 1,072?

    a. Norm Van Brocklin
    b. Pat Brady
    c. John James
    d. Jerrel Wilson
    e. Bobby Walden
    f. Sammy Baugh

32. His weekly bread basket

Going into the 1980 season Harold Carmichael of the Eagles holds the NFL record for consecutive games with at least one reception. How many games?

   a. 105
   b. 107
   c. 216
   d. 83
   e. 112
   f. 288

33. Standing on ceremony

Name the only man who has been enshrined in the Pro Football Hall of Fame, the College Football Hall of Fame, and the Baseball Hall of Fame.

   a. Hank Soar
   b. George Halas
   c. Cal Hubbard
   d. Casey Stengel
   e. Joe McCarthy
   f. Hank Sauer

34. Roll Tide roll

Pro Football Hall of Famer Don Hutson of the Green Bay Packers was one end on Alabama's 1935 Rose Bowl champions. Who was the "other" end?

   a. Dixie Howell
   b. Milt Gantenbein
   c. Paul (Bear) Bryant
   d. Max McGee
   e. Bud Wilkinson
   f. Tarzan White

Prior to the coin flip that began the first sudden death overtime period of the 1962 AFL championship game, Dallas Texans coach Hank Stram instructed captain Abner Haynes to opt for kicking off with the scoreboard clock at the Texans' backs, i.e. with the wind. In the pressure and confusion, Haynes, upon winning the toss, told the referee, "We'll kick to the clock." With that statement, Haynes in effect (however unwittingly) had attempted to exercise two options rather than the one he was allowed. Thus, "We'll kick" became Haynes's only choice, forcing Dallas to kick into the wind and taking away the advantage gained by winning the coin toss. The Texans overcame the mistake, however, and beat Houston 20–17 on a field goal by Tommy Brooker three minutes into the second overtime period.

35. Vacation job

Which former major league baseball manager quarter-backed George Halas's first pro team, the Decatur Staleys, in 1920?

    a. Casey Stengel
    b. Hugo Bezdek
    c. Charlie Dressen
    d. Walt Alston
    e. Earl Weaver
    f. Eddie Stanky

36. Mammal house

Name the seven NFL teams with animal nicknames.

As a youngster, Chicago Bears wide receiver Brian Baschnagel attended 19 different schools in 12 years.

37. The war experience helped

Name the former Marine Corps ace, Congressional Medal of Honor winner, and Governor of South Dakota who was the first AFL Commissioner.

  a. Lamar Hunt
  b. Joe Foss
  c. Joe Robbie
  d. Al Davis
  e. Milt Woodard
  f. Sid Gillman

38. Zip, zip

True or false? The 1961 and 1962 Green Bay Packers are the only teams to win back-to-back NFL championships by shutouts.

39. Tough act to follow

In his first at-bat as a major league baseball player, this Pro Football Hall of Famer set an American League record by getting a pinch-hit home run. Who is he?

  a. Carroll Hardy
  b. Sid Luckman
  c. Ken Strong
  d. Clarence (Ace) Parker
  e. Johnny Mize
  f. Paddy Driscoll

40. Who could forget?

Most NFL history buffs know that the Chicago Bears defeated the Washington Redskins 73–0 in the 1940 championsip game. However, the two teams had met three weeks prior to the championship game. What was the outcome of the earlier meeting?

a. Washington 73, Chicago 0.
b. Washington 7, Chicago 7
c. Washington 7, Chicago 3
d. Chicago 7, Washington 3
e. Chicago 21, Washington 20
f. Chicago 73, Washington 0

41. Having it both ways

Identify the only coach in pro football history to win world championships in both the AFL and NFL.

a. Weeb Ewbank
b. John Madden
c. Chuck Noll
d. Tom Landry
e. Wally Lemm
f. Ray Flaherty

42. Collection plate

Who is the former Rams fullback who used his NFL salary to finance his divinity school education?

    a. Deacon Jones
    b. Deacon Dan Towler
    c. Deacon Turner
    d. Vilnis Ezerins
    e. Don Perkins
    f. Preacher Pilot

43. It only *seemed* like the whole year

The last 0–0 tie in the NFL was between the Detroit Lions and the New York Giants. In what year was the game played?

    a. 1967
    b. 1931
    c. 1958
    d. 1943
    e. 1979
    f. 1952

44. Javelin catcher

True or false? Mike Fuller of the San Diego Chargers is the all-time NFL leader for punt return average with 11.5 yards per return.

The starting center for the Cleveland Browns when they defeated Detroit 56–10 for the 1954 NFL championship was Frank Gatski. The starting center for the Detroit Lions when they defeated Cleveland 59–14 for the 1957 NFL championship was Frank Gatski.

45. High and deep

True or false? Horace Gillom of the Cleveland Browns compiled the highest career punting average (43.8 yards) in NFL history.

46. Throwing with the right side of the brain

Who is considered the first prominent lefthanded quarterback in the pros?

a. Benny Freidman
b. Frankie Albert
c. Ken Stabler
d. Bob Waterfield
e. Jim Del Gaizo
f. Tommy Thompson

Gary Campbell, Chicago Bears outside linebacker, is a native of Hawaii. His middle name is Kalani. His daughter's is Kealiialohiokalani, which means My Shining Princess from Heaven.

47. Now, the bad news

True or false? At first it was thought that St. Louis Cardinals rookie Roy Green had set an NFL kickoff return record with a 108-yard return in 1979 against the Dallas Cowboys, but later the return yardage was officially revised downward to 106, which tied him with Al Carmichael of the Packers and Noland Smith of the Chiefs.

48. Man on a string

Which player returned more than 500 kicks (235 punt returns, 275 kickoff returns) during his 10-year career?

a. Ron Smith
b. Abe Woodson
c. George McAfee
d. Dick Bass
e. Dick Hoak
f. J.C. Caroline

49. Hard work

True or false? In 1975 Chuck Foreman accomplished the "triple crown" by leading the NFC in scoring, receiving, and rushing.

50. Favorite sons

Match the 1979 all-pro player in the first column with the college he attended in the second column.

OFFENSE

1. Dave Casper, TE		a.	Alabama A&M
2. Leon Gray, T		b.	Alabama
3. John Hannah, G		c.	USC
4. Mike Webster, C		d.	Jackson State
5. Bob Young, G		e.	Texas
6. Marvin Powell, T		f.	Notre Dame
7. John Stallworth, WR		g.	Oregon
8. John Jefferson, WR		h.	Howard Payne
9. Dan Fouts, QB		i.	Jackson State
10. Earl Campbell, RB		j.	Arizona State
11. Walter Payton, RB		k.	Wisconsin

DEFENSE

1. Lee Roy Selmon, DE		a.	Penn State
2. Randy White, DT		b.	Syracuse
3. Joe Greene, DT		c.	Maryland
4. Jack Youngblood, DE		d.	North Texas State
5. Jack Ham, LB		e.	Wisconsin-Milwaukee
6. Robert Brazile, LB		f.	Lincoln
7. Randy Gradishar, LB		g.	Florida
8. Louis Wright, CB		h.	Oklahoma
9. Lemar Parrish, CB		i.	Jackson State
10. Mike Reinfeldt, S		j.	San Jose State
11. Tommy Myers, S		k.	Ohio State

51. "Outlined against . . ."

Which of the famous Notre Dame "Four Horsemen" served as the NFL's first commissioner?

52. Throwing 'em where they ain't

Which quarterback established an NFL single-season record by being intercepted only once in 151 attempts?

a. Bart Starr
b. Joe Ferguson
c. Milt Plum
d. Ron Jaworski
e. Doug Williams
f. Jim Hardy

53. Over the table

True or false? The first known incident of a player's receiving money to play football was in 1892, when the Allegheny Athletic Association of Pittsburgh paid William (Pudge) Heffelfinger $500 for a game.

54. Isn't he from . . . ?

Match the NFL player in the first column with the school he attended in the second column.

BIG TEN

1. Mike Phipps		a. Indiana
2. Jack Rudnay		b. Iowa
3. Rod Walters		c. Michigan State
4. Joe Norman		d. Michigan
5. Don Dierdorf		e. Illinois
6. Brad Van Pelt		f. Ohio State
7. Doug France		g. Wisconsin
8. Doug Dieken		h. Northwestern
9. Mike Webster		i. Minnesota
10. Rick Upchurch		j. Purdue

PAC-10

1. Sam Cunningham		a. Arizona
2. Theotis Brown		b. Arizona State
3. Chuck Muncie		c. Oregon
4. James Lofton		d. Oregon State
5. Blair Bush		e. Washington
6. Jack Thompson		f. Washington State
7. Russ Francis		g. Stanford
8. Bob Horn		h. California
9. John Jefferson		i. UCLA
10. Mark Arneson		j. USC

BIG EIGHT

1. Greg Pruitt
2. Jon Kolb
3. Delvin Williams
4. Steve Grogan
5. Dave Logan
6. Luther Blue
7. Tony Galbreath
8. John Dutton

a. Colorado
b. Oklahoma
c. Oklahoma State
d. Kansas
e. Missouri
f. Kansas State
g. Iowa State
h. Nebraska

SOUTHWESTERN CONFERENCE

1. Jerry Sisemore
2. Pat Thomas
3. Billy Taylor
4. Riley Odoms
5. Mike Renfro
6. Wayne Morris
7. Joe Ferguson
8. Cleveland Franklin
9. Tommy Kramer

a. Rice
b. Baylor
c. Texas
d. Texas A&M
e. Texas Tech
f. Texas Christian
g. Houston
h. Arkansas
i. Southern Methodist

SOUTHEASTERN CONFERENCE

1. Tony Nathan
2. Matt Robinson
3. Dan Nugent
4. Jack Reynolds
5. Paul Hofer
6. A.J. Duhe
7. Jimmy Webb
8. Wes Chandler
9. Dennis Harrison
10. Joe Federspiel

a. Mississippi
b. Alabama
c. Vanderbilt
d. Georgia
e. Mississippi State
f. Auburn
g. Kentucky
h. Louisiana State
i. Tennessee
j. Florida

INDEPENDENTS

1.	Tom Jackson	a.	Pittsburgh
2.	Lydell Mitchell	b.	Temple
3.	Tony Dorsett	c.	Colgate
4.	Joe Theismann	d.	Louisville
5.	Mark van Eeghen	e.	Tulane
6.	Warren Bankston	f.	West Virginia
7.	Ottis Anderson	g.	Miami
8.	Tommy Myers	h.	Notre Dame
9.	Artie Owens	i.	Syracuse
10.	Joe Klecko	j.	Penn State

Contrary to modern popular thought, the first game between the NFL and the AFL took place in 1926. The New York Giants of the NFL defeated the Philadelphia Quakers 31–0. The first AFL was a league designed to showcase the talents of Red Grange.

55. Eclipsed

Which Pro Football Hall of Fame inductee was Babe Ruth's predecessor as the New York Yankees' right fielder?

   a. Lou Gehrig
   b. George Halas
   c. Paddy Driscoll
   d. Ace Parker
   e. Bobby Layne
   f. Evar Swanson

56. Part of the "baby boom"

Name the original eight teams of the All-America Football Conference of 1946.

The drop-kick made its final appearance in the NFL championship game of 1941, when Ray (Scooter) McLean scored the final point of the afternoon for the Chicago Bears in their 37–9 victory over the New York Giants.

57. Hands like leather

By carrying the ball on 369 attempts in 1979, he broke his own NFL record for carries in one season. Name the running back.

a. Earl Campbell
b. Walter Payton
c. Lydell Mitchell
d. Joe Washington
e. Chuck Muncie
f. Sam Cunningham

58. Many happy returns

True or false? Lynn Chandnois, who played with the Pittsburgh Steelers from 1950–56, is the all-time NFL kickoff return leader with an average of 29.6 yards per return.

59. Cornerstones

Which two members of Fordham University's famous line of the 1930s "The Seven Blocks of Granite," are in the Pro Football Hall of Fame?

a. Vince Lombardi and Alex Wojciechowicz
b. Vince Lombardi and Ed Franco
c. Glenn Davis and Doc Blanchard
d. Bulldog Turner and Dan Fortmann
e. Vince Lombardi and Phil Bengtson
f. Steve Filipowicz and Alex Wojciechowicz

60. Probing the legend

True or false? The 1960 Philadelphia Eagles, coached by Buck Shaw, were the only team to defeat Vince Lombardi's Green Bay Packers in a championship game.

61. Keep your head down

Who holds the NFL career record for highest field goal accuracy?

    a. Garo Yepremian
    b. Don Cockroft
    c. Tom Dempsey
    d. Bob Waterfield
    e. Bucky Dilts
    f. Pat Harder

62. Some other guy

Jim Brown holds the NFL record for most 100-yard games rushing, 58. Who is in second place with 42 games?

    a. Franco Harris
    b. Archie Griffin
    c. Tony Dorsett
    d. O.J. Simpson
    e. Walter Payton
    f. Tony Canadeo

63. Not from around here

Before moving to Washington, what city did the Redskins call home?

    a. Atlanta
    b. Boston
    c. Chicago
    d. Detroit
    e. Easton
    f. Frankford

64. Courted, then netted

In the 1960s, the Dallas Cowboys, who have built a reputation for finding players in unorthodox places, fie'ded two starters who had played no college football but had been basketball players as collegians. Who were they?

    a. Walt Garrison and Chuck Howley
    b. Pete Gent and Mel Renfro
    c. Don Perkins and Cornell Green
    d. Walt Garrison and Mel Renfro
    e. Chuck Howley and Mel Renfro
    f. Pete Gent and Cornell Green

At the start of the 1979 NFL season, the San Diego Chargers' roster showed three names of former and present major league baseball players: running back Hank Bauer, quarterback Dave Rader, and center Bob Rush.

65. "The invisible team"

True of false? There are eight officials in an NFL crew.

66. *Now,* may we go home?

Who kicked the field goal in the second overtime period
to win the 1962 AFL title for the Dallas Texans?

   a. George Blanda
   b. Abner Haynes
   c. Lamar Hunt
   d. Lou Groza
   e. Tommy Brooker
   f. Bill Shockley

*The first televised pro football game took place on Octo-
ber 22, 1939 at Brooklyn's Ebbets Field. The Brooklyn
Dodgers defeated the Philadelphia Eagles 23–14, and the
game was carried by NBC, which used two cameras, one
at field level and one on the mezzanine. Announcer Allan
(Skip) Walz was his own spotter and used hand signals to
direct the cameraman to the appropriate game action.*

67. A lost art

Which member of the Pro Football Hall of Fame is considered "the last of the great drop-kickers?"

a. Lou Groza
b. George Blanda
c. Dutch Clark
d. Jim Bakken
e. Sammy Baugh
f. Doak Walker

68. Let's see, that's three gallons of blue . . .

Name the NFL general manager who, as a player, designed the first helmet logo—for the Los Angeles Rams in 1948—then painted the team's entire supply of headgear.

a. Bob Waterfield
b. Bucko Kilroy
c. Fred Gehrke
d. Norm Van Brocklin
e. Jim Finks
f. Don Klosterman

69. Receptive

Who holds the NFL career record for most receptions, 649?

  a. Raymond Berry
  b. Don Maynard
  c. Lionel Taylor
  d. Dan Abramowicz
  e. Harold Carmichael
  f. Charley Taylor

70. Pickpocket

True or false? Emlen Tunnell, who played with the New York Giants and Green Bay Packers, is the all-time NFL interception leader.

71. They "used him up"

Which running back holds the NFL record for the most rushing attempts in a game, 41?

  a. Terdell Middleton, Packers
  b. Earl Campbell, Oilers
  c. O.J. Simpson, 49ers
  d. John Riggins, Redskins
  e. Franco Harris, Steelers
  f. Harry Newman, Giants

72. Without starting blocks

Identify the former Olympic gold medal-winning sprinter who once scored on a 101-yard interception return.

  a. Bob Hayes
  b. Ollie Matson
  c. Homer Jones
  d. Doak Walker
  e. Henry Carr
  f. Gerald Tinker

73. The human pendulum

Name the kicker who holds the NFL record for most field goals in a season, 34.

  a. Lou Michaels
  b. Sonny Jurgensen
  c. Jack Manders
  d. Jim Turner
  e. Roy Gerela
  f. Ward Cuff

74. Me DEE-fense

Name the former NFL linebacker who played Tarzan in films in the 1960s.

a. Buster Crabbe
b. Burt Reynolds
c. Lee Majors
d. Mike Henry
e. Tim Rossovich
f. Johnny Mack Brown

Don't be fooled by this bogus trivia question: In 1963, the most valuable players of the National Football League, the American Football League, and baseball's American and National Leagues all wore the same number. What was it? Well, it wasn't one number. The bogus answer is 32, which was in fact the number worn by Jim Brown (NFL), Elston Howard (AL), and Sandy Koufax (NL). But the AFL's most valuable player, Clem Daniels of the Oakland Raiders, wore 36. Tough question, though.

75. No. 1 in their hearts

Which jersey number was issued to O.J. Simpson when he reported to the Buffalo Bills in 1969?

    a. 32
    b. 9
    c. 00
    d. 36
    e. 7
    f. 30

76. Spiral showcase

The NFL record for longest punt (98 yards) may never be broken. Who holds it?

    a. Sammy Baugh
    b. Yale Lary
    c. Horace Gillom
    d. Tom Blanchard
    e. Steve O'Neal
    f. Tommy Davis

The first player to use eyeglasses during an NFL game was Baltimore receiver Raymond Berry, who wore shaded swimmer's goggles to protect against the winter sun in the Los Angeles Coliseum in the late 1950s and early 1960s.

77. Air travel

Dan Fouts of the San Diego Chargers passed for a record-setting total of 4,082 yards in 1979. Who is the only other NFI quarterback to surpass the 4,000 yard mark in a single season?

a. Sonny Jurgensen
b. Terry Bradshaw
c. Dan Pastorini
d. Fran Tarkenton
e. Joe Namath
f. Jim Hart

78. Key player

Name the former Pro Bowl defensive tackle who retired abruptly in 1974 to devote full time to his career as a pianist?

a. Merlin Olsen
b. Bob Lilly
c. Mike Reid
d. Bill Kollar
e. Willie Lanier
f. Jethro Pugh

79. Rip and run

Which defensive back holds the career record for returning interceptions for the most career touchdowns (9)?

   a. Lem Barney
   b. Ken Houston
   c. Jack Butler
   d. Dick (Night Train) Lane
   e. Will Sherman
   f. Milt Davis

80. Track meet

The highest scoring game in NFL history was played in 1966 between the Washington Redskins and the New York Giants. What was the score?

   a. 73–0
   b. 47–45
   c. 101–28
   d. 68–14
   e. 86–21
   f. 72–41

81. Dodge 'em

True or false? In 1979 Rick Upchurch of the Broncos surpassed Emlen Tunnell as the NFL's all-time leader for punt return yardage (2,288).

82. No stopping him

The record for the most points scored by an individual in an NFL game (40) has stood since 1929. Who holds the record?

a. George Halas
b. Ernie Nevers
c. Dub Jones
d. Dutch Clark
e. Clarke Hinkle
f. Hinkey Haines

83. Complementary

True or false? Jim and Jack Youngblood of the Rams are the only twins playing in the NFL.

84. Fast break

Who was the first NFL running back to rush for more than a thousand yards in each of his first three seasons?

a. Franco Harris
b. O.J. Simpson
c. Walter Payton
d. John Brockington
e. Larry Brown
f. Byron (Whizzer) White

The term "Red Dog," the original nickname for the defensive gambit now known as the blitz, came from the first man to attempt one: Don (Red) Ettinger, a linebacker for the New York Giants from 1948–50. With the offensive team in a third-and-long situation, Ettinger left his normal position and sacked the quarterback for a substantial loss. "I had red hair, and I was just doggin' the quarterback a little," he explained later.

85. Popular title

True or false? The American Football League (1960–69) was the fourth NFL rival to be so named.

86. Back it up

Name the NFL running back who was credited with a
1,000-yard season after a review of films showed that what
had been called lost yardage was really a fumble and
should not have been subtracted from his total.

a. Mercury Morris
b. Duane Thomas
c. Larry Csonka
d. O.J. Simpson
e. Jim Kiick
f. Don Perkins

The first President of the United States to attend a Mon-
day Night Football game was Jimmy Carter, who watched
Washington defeat Dallas 9–5 in 1978.

87. Extra credit for "Wahoo"

Match the player in the first column with his nickname in the second column.

1. Red Grange
2. Ted Hendricks
3. Alex Karras
4. Elroy Hirsch
5. Clyde Turner
6. Ron McDole
7. Frank Kinard
8. Daryle Lamonica
9. Leo Nomellini
10. Glenn Edwards

a. The Dancing Bear
b. Turk
c. Mad Duck
d. The Mad Stork
e. Bruiser
f. The Lion
g. The Galloping Ghost
h. Crazylegs
i. The Mad Bomber
j. Bulldog

88. The aviary

Name the four NFL teams with bird nicknames.

89. Double centuries

Name the player who recorded more 200-yard games rushing (six) than any other running back in NFL history.

a. Walter Payton
b. John Fuqua
c. O.J. Simpson
d. Jim Brown
e. Earl Campbell
f. Mike Thomas

90. Going the extra mile

Who is the only NFL running back to gain more than 2,000 yards in a season?

a. Ottis Anderson
b. Jim Brown
c. Franco Harris
d. Abe Woodson
e. Walter Payton
f. O.J. Simpson

91. Taking the bitter with the sweet

Which quarterback holds the NFL records for most touchdown passes (36) in a season and most interceptions in a season (42)?

a. Greg Cook
b. Ken Anderson
c. George Blanda
d. Fran Tarkenton
e. Norman Snead
f. Sid Luckman

92. Home of champions

Which team has won the most NFL championships?

   a. Chicago Bears
   b. Green Bay Packers
   c. Dallas Cowboys
   d. Canton Bulldogs
   e. Detroit Lions
   f. Atlanta Falcons

93. Reigning runner

Which running back led the NFL in rushing in 1979?

   a. O.J. Simpson
   b. Franco Harris
   c. Ottis Anderson
   d. Terdell Middleton
   e. Earl Campbell
   f. Chuck Foreman

94. That'll cost you . . .

Which team was assessed the most penalty yardage in one game, 209?

   a. Atlanta Falcons
   b. Baltimore Colts
   c. Cleveland Browns
   d. Dallas Cowboys
   e. Philadelphia Eagles
   f. Frankford Yellowjackets

95. "It's up, it's . . ."

Who holds the NFL record for the longest field goal?

    a. Bruce Alford
    b. Lou Groza
    c. Paddy Driscoll
    d. Tom Dempsey
    e. Jack Manders
    f. Gene Mingo

Earl Morrall was acquired by the Baltimore Colts for the 1968 season as an "insurance" quarterback. Johnny Unitas was injured during much of the regular season. Morrall started against, and beat, each of his former teams that season:
    Colts 27, San Francisco 10
    Colts 41, Pittsburgh 7
    Colts 42, San Francisco 14
    Colts 26, New York Giants 0
    Colts 27, Detroit 10

96. Born to lose

Which NFL team lost the most consecutive games?

- a. Detroit Lions
- b. Oakland Raiders
- c. San Francisco 49ers
- d. Philadelphia Eagles
- e. Los Angeles Rams
- f. Tampa Bay Buccaneers

97. The last of the great quintuple-threats

Who holds the NFL record for the most combined yards gained (rushing, receiving, punt returns, kickoff returns, and fumble returns) in a season?

- a. Bruce Harper
- b. Timmy Brown
- c. Terry Metcalf
- d. Mack Herron
- e. Bobby Mitchell
- f. Walter Payton

Walter Payton's marriage gave him another bond with his college (Jackson State) teammate and best friend, Rickey Young of the Vikings. Young's wife Hazel and Mrs. Payton (Connie) are aunt and niece, making Young Payton's uncle by marriage.

98. Pioneer

Who was the first modern-day black quarterback in the NFL?

a. Marlin Briscoe
b. Eldridge Dickey
c. Joe Gilliam
d. Willie Thrower
e. James Harris
f. Doug Williams

99. You gotta be a football hero

Who is the baseball player and manager who was a star runner at Louisiana State in the 1940s while Pro Football Hall of Famer Steve Van Buren was used as a blocking back?

a. Charlie Conerly
b. Alvin Dark
c. Lloyd Merriman
d. Casey Stengel
e. Vic Janowicz
f. Bill Dickey

100. Gift of prophecy

Jeanne Dixon, a noted psychic, is the sister of which famous football player?

   a. Bob Waterfield
   b. Bobby Layne
   c. Hewritt Dixon
   d. Paul Dickson
   e. Cliff Battles
   f. Erny Pinckert

101. Stay tuned

Which linebacker had a role in a 1979 episode of the daytime drama (they used to call them soap operas) "One Life to Live"?

   a. Jack Lambert
   b. Bill Bergey
   c. Randy Gradishar
   d. Greg Buttle
   e. Brad Van Pelt
   f. Harry Carson

102. Made to be broken

Which quarterback broke Fran Tarkenton's records for the most passing attempts and completions in a season in 1979?

    a. Steve DeBerg
    b. Roger Staubach
    c. Pat Haden
    d. Terry Bradshaw
    e. Archie Manning
    f. Jim Zorn

103. Mr. Consistency

Who holds the record for most times leading the NFL in rushing?

    a. O.J. Simpson
    b. Walter Payton
    c. Jim Brown
    d. Tony Canadeo
    e. Steve Van Buren
    f. Bill Paschal

104. Packing the pigskin to paydirt

Which Pro Football Hall of Fame halfback/flanker holds the record for scoring a touchdown in 18 consecutive games?

    a. Jim Brown
    b. Jim Taylor
    c. Gale Sayers
    d. Hugh McElhenny
    e. Don Hutson
    f. Lenny Moore

105. Just sign here, son

Who were the two Dallas Cowboys stars signed to personal services contracts and dealt for, rather than drafted, in 1960?

    a. Eddie LeBaron and Bill Howton
    b. Bob Lilly and Bob Hayes
    c. Don Perkins and Don Meredith
    d. Lee Roy Jordan and Jerry Tubbs
    e. Amos Marsh and Mel Renfro
    f. Frank Clarke and Chuck Howley

In 1957 the Philadelphia Eagles drafted the following players:

Round 1, Clarence Peaks, Michigan State.
Round 2, Billy Ray Barnes, Wake Forest.
Round 3, Tommy McDonald, Oklahoma.
Round 4, Sonny Jurgensen, Duke.

In the early 1960s, the quartet comprised the starting backfield, with Jurgensen at quarterback, Barnes at halfback, Peaks at fullback, and McDonald at flanker.

106. When in doubt ...

Which punter failed prior tryouts with the New York Jets, but made it with the Kansas City Chiefs in 1979 and led the NFL in punting?

a. Steve O'Neal
b. Jerrel Wilson
c. Bucky Dilts
d. Chuck Ramsey
e. Zenon Andrusyshyn
f. Bob Grupp

107. Something to kick about

Which NFL umpire shares the record for kicking the most extra points (nine) in a game?

a. Frank Sinkovitz
b. Jim Tunney
c. Dean Look
d. Lou Groza
e. Pat Harder
f. Tommy Davis

While playing quarterback in the NFL, Charley Johnson and Frank Ryan earned Ph.D.s. Johnson's was in chemical engineering, Ryan's in mathematics.

108. Draft-dodgers

The Washington Redskins chose Art Monk, a wide receiver from Syracuse, on the first round of the 1980 draft. It was the first time in years that they had kept their number one pick. Who had been their last first round choice?

a. Ray McDonald, 1967
b. Jim (Yazoo) Smith, 1968
c. Bill Brundige, 1970
d. Moses Denson, 1972
e. Mike Thomas, 1975
f. John Riggins, 1976

109. If it's moving, fall on it

Who holds the record for the most opponents' fumbles recovered in a season?

a. Corwin Clatt
b. Chuck Howley
c. Don Hultz
d. Joe Schmidt
e. Dick Butkus
f. Jim Marshall

110. They *shall* pass

Which is the only team in the 61-year history of the NFL to attempt more than 600 passes?

   a. New York Giants, 1961
   b. Dallas Cowboys, 1967
   c. Green Bay Packers, 1936
   d. San Francisco 49ers, 1979
   e. Houston Oilers, 1965
   f. New York Jets, 1968

111. Ground pounders

Which is the only team to have four players gain more than 500 yards rushing in the same season?

   a. New England Patriots, 1978
   b. Pittsburgh Steelers, 1976
   c. Detroit Lions, 1974
   d. Green Bay Packers, 1961
   e. Miami Dolphins, 1972
   f. Oakland Raiders, 1979

112. Super coverage

True or false? Super Bowl I was televised by two networks, ABC and NBC.

113. Tool of ignorance

What was the nickname of the Kansas City Chiefs' defensive back who predicted dire results for the Packers in Super Bowl I?

    a. Brother Sledge
    b. The Hatchet
    c. Stinger
    d. Motor Mouth
    e. The Hammer
    f. Crash

114. On his toes

Who kicked four field goals to help the Green Bay Packers win Super Bowl II?

    a. Paul Hornung
    b. Jerry Kramer
    c. Don Chandler
    d. Mike Eischeid
    e. Jim Taylor
    f. Ron Widby

115. Holding on to it

Name the man who shares the record for the most touchdowns in a Super Bowl game, having caught two scoring passes in Super Bowl II.

    a. Glenn Bass
    b. Bill Miller
    c. Harry Schuh
    d. Chuck Mercein
    e. Bob Long
    f. Bob Tucker

116. Audacity spoken here

True or false? Except for the Green Bay Packers in Super Bowl I, the New York Jets are the only team to win a Super Bowl game in their first attempt.

U.S. Supreme Court Justice Byron (Whizzer) White not only led the NFL in rushing two out of the three years he played, he is the only player ever to have done it with two different teams. White gained 567 yards with the Pittsburgh Pirates in 1938. He spent the next year at Oxford University as a Rhodes Scholar, then returned to pro football as a member of the Detroit Lions. In 1940, he gained 514 yards, again winning the rushing title. He retired after the 1941 season.

117. Out of sight

Near the end of the first half of Super Bowl III, quarter-back Earl Morrall of the Baltimore Colts had a receiver wide open in the end zone on a gadget play. Morrall did not see him and attempted to throw to a closer man. The ball was intercepted. Who was the man left standing in the end zone, waving his arms?

    a. Tom Matte
    b. Randy Beverly
    c. Jimmy Orr
    d. John Mackey
    e. George Sauer, Jr.
    f. Pettis Norman

118. Masochist

True or false? Fran Tarkenton was the starting quarter-back in all four of the Minnesota Vikings' Super Bowl losses.

Throughout his career Johnny Unitas's flattop haircut and high-top shoes were as much trademarks as his jersey number 19. For Super Bowl V, Unitas presented a new image—long hair and low-cut shoes.

119. Mumbo jumbo

Kansas City head coach Hank Stram had a special name for the multiple offensive formations he used in Super Bowl IV. What was it?

a. The 65 Toss Power Trap Series
b. The Belly Series
c. The Offense of the Seventies
d. The Bazooka
e. The Peg-leg T
f. The Kansas City Strip

120. Helping hand

The longest touchdown reception in Super Bowl history was a controversial one. In Super Bowl V it was ruled that a Dallas defender tipped the ball after it had been touched by the original intended receiver (Eddie Hinton) but before John Mackey caught it to complete the 75-yard play. Name the defensive back who was ruled to have touched the ball.

a. Mel Renfro
b. Tom Maxwell
c. Cornell Green
d. Charlie Waters
e. Herb Adderley
f. Rick Volk

121. Silent partner

Although he did not win player of the game honors, which running back had an outstanding day (19 carries for 95 yards and one touchdown) for the winners of Super Bowl VI?

    a. Jim Kiick
    b. Duane Thomas
    c. Larry Csonka
    d. Walt Garrison
    e. Robert Newhouse
    f. Mercury Morris

122. Out-of-town dudes

Both of Roger Staubach's touchdown passes in Super Bowl VI were caught by players who had spent the majority of their careers with teams other than the Cowboys. Name the pair of not-so-old cowhands.

    a. Paul Warfield and Billy Howton
    b. Gloster Richardson and Billy Truax
    c. Tommy McDonald and Ron Sellers
    d. Lance Alworth and Mike Ditka
    e. Margene Adkins and Richmond Flowers
    f. Reggie Rucker and Halvor Hagen

123. Peak performance

Which defensive lineman had a "once-in-a-lifetime" game in Super Bowl VII?

   a. Manny Sistrunk
   b. Otis Sistrunk
   c. Bob Heinz
   d. Manny Fernandez
   e. Larry Ball
   f. John Wilbur

124. Not in the playbook

Field goal placements usually follow a certain format: snap, hold, kick. In Super Bowl VII, Garo Yepremian, the Dolphins' kicker, did something that made the game more exciting. What was it?

   a. He kicked barefooted.
   b. After a blocked field goal attempt, he attempted a pass that turned into a fumble and was run back for a Redskins touchdown.
   c. He drop-kicked a 43-yard field goal.
   d. He kicked one extra point with his right foot and another with his left.
   e. He ran for an extra point after faking a kick.
   f. He passed for an extra point.

125. A ring for each finger

True or false? Marv Fleming is the only man to play in five Super Bowls—I and II with the Packers, and VI, VII, and VIII with the Dolphins.

126. Grounded

Rushing was the key to winning Super Bowl IX. The
Steelers gained 249 yards on the ground, while the Vikings managed considerably fewer. What was the Vikings'
net rushing yardage?

   a. Minus-47 yards
   b. 117 yards
   c. 187 yards
   d. 17 yards
   e. 44 yards
   f. 93 yards.

*One player not disturbed by media attention accompany-
ing Super Bowl IX was Pittsburgh Steelers center Ray
Mansfield. Said the 33-year-old veteran of the Steelers'
lean years, "I've been in this league for twelve seasons,
and no one's ever asked me a question."*

127. Understudies

Two of the Steelers' all-pro linebackers—Andy Russell and Jack Lambert—missed much of Super Bowl IX due to injuries. Which two young linebackers took their places?

   a. Loren Toews and Ed Bradley
   b. Mike Webster and Marv Kellum
   c. Jack Ham and Marv Kellum
   d. Dick Conn and Jim Allen
   e. Reggie Harrison and Robin Cole
   f. Doug Fisher and Ray May

128. Reeling with excitement

Which movie used Super Bowl X as a backdrop?

   a. Bad Day at Black Rock
   b. Black Sunday
   c. Semi-Tough
   d. North Dallas Forty
   e. The Longest Yard
   f. Crazylegs II

President Richard M. Nixon, whose Florida "White House" was located at Key Biscayne, sent Dolphins head coach Don Shula a play for use in Super Bowl VI. The following year Nixon sent a play to George Allen of the Redskins even though the Dolphins were again in the Super Bowl. Nixon claimed that the Redskins were "really my 'home team.'"

129. Journeyman

True or false? Preston Pearson has appeared in five Super Bowls with five different teams: Colts, Vikings, Steelers, Chiefs, and Cowboys.

130. Magnetizer

True or false? Though he scored no touchdowns in Super Bowl XI, Fred Biletnikoff's four receptions for 79 yards earned him the game's most valuable player award.

131. Icing

Which defensive back returned an interception 75 yards for a touchdown to give Oakland its final points in Super Bowl XI?

    a. Jack Tatum
    b. George Atkinson
    c. Willie Brown
    d. Alonzo (Skip) Thomas
    e. Neal Colzie
    f. Nate Allen

132. Maiden voyage

True or false? Red Miller took the Denver Broncos to Super Bowl XII in his first year as head coach of the team.

133. X's and O's going everywhere

Which "gadget play" gave the Dallas Cowboys their final touchdown in Super Bowl XII?

    a. A Statue of Liberty play with Tony Dorsett going 43 yards.
    b. A running back-option pass from Robert Newhouse to Golden Richards.
    c. A 27-yard pass from holder Danny White to field goal kicker Efren Herrera.
    d. A Staubach-to-Dorsett-to-Preston-Pearson-to-Dorsett-back-to-Staubach-to-DuPree flea-flicker.
    e. A Dorsett-to-Staubach pass.
    f. A 27-yard run by field goal kicker Efren Herrera.

134. Doomsday duo

What distinction do Harvey Martin and Randy White share?

   a. They are the only two defensive players to receive Super Bowl most valuable player honors.

   b. They are the only Cowboys to win Super Bowl most valuable player honors.

   c. They are the only players named co-most valuable players in a Super Bowl.

   d. They are the only two most valuable players who did not play quarterback.

   e. They both scored touchdowns on fumble returns in Super Bowl XII.

   f. They both started in Super Bowl XII as rookies.

135. Automatic milestone

True or false? Either team in Super Bowl XIII—the Pittsburgh Steelers or Dallas Cowboys—would have become the first to win three Super Bowls.

136. Easily bored

True or false? Larry Cole of the Dallas Cowboys has started three Super Bowls at three different positions.

For Super Bowl XIII, the catering service that contracted with the Orange Bowl ordered the following: four tons of hot dogs, 100 pounds of cheese, 30,000 hamburgers, 1,000 heads of cabbage for sauerkraut, four tons of ice, 15,000 gallons of soda, 1,500 pounds of french fries, 15,000 ice cream sandwiches, and 3,000 gallons of coffee.

137. Hanging on

True or false? The Steelers and Rams combined to set two records in Super Bowl XIV—most yards passing, both teams (503) and fewest fumbles, both teams (0).

138. High profiles

Seven of the 14 Super Bowl most valuable player awards have been won by five quarterbacks. Who are they?

a. Bart Starr, Joe Namath, Len Dawson, Fran Tarkenton, and Roger Staubach.

b. Roger Staubach, Terry Bradshaw, Joe Kapp, Len Dawson, and Bart Starr.

c. Bart Starr, Joe Namath, Len Dawson, Roger Staubach, and Terry Bradshaw.

d. Bart Starr, Joe Namath, Len Dawson, Terry Bradshaw, and Bob Griese.

e. Bart Starr, Joe Namath, Ken Stabler, Joe Kapp, and Vince Ferragamo.

f. Bart Starr, Joe Namath, Len Dawson, Terry Bradshaw, and Dan Pastorini.

Larry Ball was a reserve linebacker with the Miami Dolphins in 1972 when they went 17–0 in 1972 (including a victory in Super Bowl VII) and with the Tampa Bay Buccaneers when they went 0–14 in 1976.

139. Shadow figure

Which of the following was the first Super Bowl most valuable player who was *not* a quarterback?

   a. Jan Stenerud
   b. Mercury Morris
   c. Lynn Swann
   d. Chuck Howley
   e. Bob Lilly
   f. Joe Greene

140. Running away with it

Which pair of running backs are the only two to be named most valuable players in the Super Bowl?

   a. Tony Dorsett and Franco Harris
   b. Duane Thomas and Walt Garrison
   c. Larry Csonka and Tony Dorsett
   d. Franco Harris and Larry Csonka
   e. Mike Garrett and Wendell Tyler
   f. Chuck Foreman and Dave Osborn

141. Show-stoppers

True or false? The only defensive players to have received the Super Bowl's most valuable player award were members of the Dallas Cowboys.

142. Receivers, recipients

True or false? Lynn Swann and John Stallworth are the only two receivers to win most valuable player awards in the Super Bowl.

143. Tough talk

Who originated the quote "40 for 60," which means 40 men (the team) for 60 minutes (the length of a game)?

a. Fran Tarkenton
b. Ken Stabler
c. Len Dawson
d. Joe Kapp
e. Terry Bradshaw
f. Bart Starr

144. Mystery men

What do the following men have in common? Mike Mercer, Bill Miller, Tom Nowatzke, Mike Bass, Dwight White, Percy Howard, Stu Voigt, Mike Hegman, and Ron Smith.

a. They were all free agents who made it to the Super Bowl.
b. Each scored in a Super Bowl.
c. They all played on losing Super Bowl teams.
d. They all were released by one Super Bowl team and acquired by another.
e. They all played college football at Grambling.
f. They all played in three or more Super Bowls.

145. Two by two

True or false? The only two safeties recorded in Super Bowl history are both credited to Pittsburgh Steelers.

146. Repetitious

True or false? Vince Lombardi, Don Shula, Tom Landry, and Chuck Noll each won back-to-back Super Bowls.

Veteran NFL field judge Bob Wortman has officiated two Super Bowls (VI and XII) and two NCAA basketball finals (UCLA vs. Kentucky in 1975 and Indiana vs. Michigan in 1976).

147. Over-the-hill gang(s)?

True or false? George Allen is the only coach in NFL history to take two different teams to the Super Bowl.

148. Sticky fingers

True or false? The leading interceptor in Super Bowl history is a free safety.

It is safe to say that the Miami Dolphins' game plan for Super Bowl VIII stressed ball control. In their 24–7 victory over Minnesota, they scored on three of their first four possessions and at one point led 24–0. Dolphins running back Larry Csonka set a Super Bowl rushing record with 145 yards in 33 carries, and quarterback Bob Griese attempted only seven passes, completing six for 73 yards.

149. Sacrificial lamb

True or false? Tom Landry has been in more Super Bowls than any other head coach, but he also has lost more.

150. Flying north in winter

True or false? The Silverdome in Pontiac, Michigan, in 1982 will be the first Super Bowl site outside the Los Angeles, Miami, or New Orleans areas.

You Make the Call

The job of officiating an NFL game is anything but trivial. Proof of this is always fresh in the mind. It's as recent as the last crucial playoff game, where a whole season can appear to hang on a single call. So if the sub-atomic-sized details of the rule book can take on such mighty significance, what are they doing in this sea of minutiae? The answer is part of the question: an eye for detail brings the game into sharper focus. Whether the data you're gathering *seems* important or not, it's always worth storing for possible future use. With that in mind, and with one hand on your penalty flag, pay close attention to the next 30 situations (all of which actually took place). Our thanks go to their author, Norm Schachter, a former NFL official and currently an observer of officials for the league. For an instantly replayed unraveling of the problems, turn to page 172.

1. Opening number

On the opening kickoff of a game between San Diego and Seattle, the Chargers' return man catches the ball in his end zone and fumbles it there after taking a step or two. The ball rolls out to the 2-yard line, where a San Diego teammate recovers it and runs to midfield before being tackled by a Seattle player. During the fumble, while the ball is on the 2, a San Diego player clips one of the Seahawks at the 8-yard line. What would you rule?

a. San Diego's ball, first and 10 at the Chargers' 4.
b. San Diego's ball, first and 10 at the Chargers' 1.
c. Re-kick from the 50-yard line (penalize San Diego 15 yards and replay the kickoff).
d. Safety against San Diego, Chargers kick off from their 20.

2. Good deed for the day?

Baltimore has the ball on New England's 40-yard line, third down and 15. The Baltimore quarterback throws a look-in pass to his tight end. The ball goes off the tight end's hands at New England's 30-yard line and pops right into the hands of a New England cornerback. He runs the interception back to Baltimore's 20, and the Baltimore quarterback is the only man left who can tackle the runner. The cornerback avoids the quarterback but slips and falls without being touched. A New England teammate running alongside to block sees the cornerback slip. He reaches over and helps the ball carrier to his feet at Baltimore's 20-yard line. He then blocks the Colts' quarterback at the Baltimore 10-yard line, allowing the cornerback to go in for a score. How would you rule?

    a. Touchdown.
    b. New England's ball, first down at Baltimore's 35-yard line.
    c. New England's ball, first down at Baltimore's 25-yard line.
    d. New England's ball, first down at Baltimore's 15-yard line.

3. This will only take a second

Dallas has the ball on its own 4-yard line, second down and 15. The Cowboys' quarerback hands off to his running back, who fumbles. The ball rolls backward, into Dallas's end zone. A Detroit defensive tackle pushes the Cowboys' quarterback out of the way, and a Lions' teammate recovers the ball in the end zone. How would you rule?

a. Touchdown for Detroit.
b. Touchback for Dallas.
c. Dallas's ball, first down at its own 9-yard line (after penalizing Detroit five yards from the spot of the previous snap for illegal use of hands).
d. Dallas's ball, first down at its own 19-yard line (after penalizing Detroit 15 yards from the spot of the previous snap for illegal use of hands).

4. Echoes of another era

Dallas leads the New York Giants by two points with a minute left to play. The Giants' placekicker prepares for a field goal attempt from the Dallas 12-yard line. As he kicks the ball with his right foot, a Dallas defensive tackle comes crashing through and blocks the ball with his chest. The ball bounces back to the kicker's left, and as it bounces, he kicks it with his left foot. It goes over the crossbar, and the crowd goes wild. The official blows his whistle and throws his flag. The players rush him and ask why. He says, "I don't know what it is, but I know it's wrong." A few seconds later, he announces his decision. Which of these rulings should it be?

   a. Field goal.
   b. Touchback.
   c. Penalize the Giants 15 yards from the spot of the snap.
   d. Penalize the Giants 15 yards from the spot of the second kick.

5. The old greased pig play

Washington has the ball, third down and 14, on its own 4-yard line. The Redskins' quarterback fakes a handoff to his running back, then drops back into his own end zone. He is blindsided by a Dallas tackler, and the ball pops out of his hands. The ball scoots toward the sideline and is angling out of the end zone. It reaches Washington's 1-yard line when the Redskins' running back tries to fall on it, but it squirts away and hits the shaft of the goal line marker. A Dallas player then falls on the ball in the end zone. What would you rule?

   a. Touchdown for Dallas.
   b. Safety against Washington.
   c. Touchback for Washington.
   d. Washington's ball on its own 1-yard line, fourth down.

6. Not part of the script

San Francisco has the ball on its own 15-yard line, second down and 15. The 49ers' quarterback rolls out and looks downfield for an eligible receiver. He is being chased, and he runs past the line of scrimmage to his 16-yard line, where he tries to throw a backward pass to his running back. The pass goes forward instead of backward. An Eagles linebacker bats the ball back toward the 49ers' end zone. The ball lands in the end zone, where the linebacker falls on it. What would you rule?

    a. Touchdown.
    b. 49ers' ball, first and 10 from their 31.
    c. 49ers' ball, third and 19 from their 11.
    d. 49ers' ball, third and 15 from their 15.

7. Flying low

Atlanta has just scored. With less than two minutes to go, the Falcons now trail the New York Jets by only two points. The Atlanta kicker attempts an onside kick, but the ball goes only eight yards before being touched by a Jets player. The ball then is touched, in turn, by an Atlanta player, a Jets player, and another Atlanta player. It is finally recovered by an Atlanta player on the Falcons' 45-yard line, with one of his feet touching the sideline at the 46. How would you rule it?

a. Atlanta's ball on its own 45.
b. Atlanta's ball on its own 46.
c. Re-kick with a five-yard penalty against Atlanta.
d. Jets' ball on Atlanta's 45-yard line.

8. Overjoyed

Minnesota is having trouble moving the ball against Detroit. It is third down for the Vikings at their own 10-yard line. The Vikings' quarterback scrambles around in his backfield and finally unloads a long pass to his wide receiver, who catches the ball at midfield. The receiver runs toward Detroit's goal line. When he reaches the Lions' 5, he mistakes it for the goal line. He spikes the ball from the 5. It hits on the 4 and rolls into Detroit's end zone, where a Detroit player falls on it. How would you rule it?

   a. Award a touchback to Detroit.
   b. Minnesota's ball on Detroit's 5-yard line, first down.
   c. Minnesota's ball on Detroit's 10-yard line, first down.
   d. Minnesota's ball on Detroit's 10-yard line, second down.

9. Lost in traffic

The Chicago Bears have the ball on third down at midfield. A Bears' running back takes a handoff and runs to the Vikings' 40-yard line, where he fumbles into a crowd of players. A Minnesota player picks up the ball but, due to confusion, runs toward his own goal line. Just as he crosses the goal line, he throws the ball down in front of himself. The ball hits in the end zone and bounces out to the Minnesota 2-yard line, where a Chicago player picks up the ball and runs it in. What would you rule?

    a. Touchdown for the Bears.
    b. Touchback for the Vikings.
    c. Safety against the Vikings.
    d. Bears' ball on the Vikings' 2-yard line.

10. All-star aberration

In a Pro Bowl game, the NFC has the ball on the AFC's 30-yard line. The NFC quarterback drops back to pass and throws a beauty to his wide receiver, who catches it on the AFC's 4-yard line. When the wide receiver reaches the 3, one of the AFC defenders reaches up, grabs him by the face mask, and flips him forward. The receiver hits the ground on the 2 but drops the ball before he lands. The ball rolls into the end zone and over the end line. How would you call it?

a. Touchdown for the NFC.
b. Touchdown for the NFC and a 15-yard penalty against the AFC on the next kickoff.
c. NFC's ball, first down on the AFC's 1-yard line.
d. NFC's ball, first down on the AFC's 2-yard line.

11. High rate of exchange

On the opening kickoff of a game between Los Angeles and Atlanta, the Rams' return man catches the ball on his own 10-yard line and runs toward his left on a criss-cross pattern. He hands the ball forward to a teammate at his 15-yard line. At the 16, the new ball carrier is tackled and fumbles. An Atlanta defender recovers at the 16, then runs the ball into the Rams' end zone. How would you rule it?

    a. Touchdown for Atlanta.
    b. Atlanta's ball, first and 10 from the Rams' 16.
    c. Rams' ball, first and 10 from their 16.
    d. Rams' ball, first and 10 from their 10.

12. Variations on a theme of rejection

On fourth down with the ball on the 50-yard line, Oakland's punter takes the snap at his own 38. A Los Angeles lineman breaks through and blocks the punt. The ball rolls to the Raiders' 30, with one Ram and one Raider chasing it. The Ram uses his hands to push the Raider out of the way, then picks up the ball and runs it into Oakland's end zone. How would you rule it?

a. Touchdown for Los Angeles.
b. Rams' ball, first and 10 from Oakland's 30.
c. Raiders' ball, first and 10 from their 35.
d. Raiders' ball, first and 10 from their 45.

13. Zero for artistry

On second and 10 from his own 10-yard line, the Saints' quarterback takes the snap and rolls out to his right. He crosses the line of scrimmage and goes to the 11, where he throws a forward pass to his wide receiver. As the receiver reaches up for the ball at his 30-yard line, a Rams defensive back pushes him away from the ball, intercepts it, and runs into New Orleans's end zone. What would you rule?

    a. Defensive pass interference, Saints' ball at their 30.
    b. Touchdown for Los Angeles.
    c. Saints' ball, third and 14 from their 6.
    d. Re-play the down, because both teams fouled on the play.

14. Guess the location

Chicago kicks off to Baltimore. The ball goes 15 yards downfield to the 50. A strong wind then catches the ball in midair and blows it back toward Chicago's 30-yard line. One of the Chicago players falls on it at the 30. Keep in mind that the ball has traveled 15 yards forward before being blown back. What would you rule?

  a. Chicago's ball, first and 10 from its 30.
  b. Re-kick, with a five-yard penalty against Chicago for a short free kick.
  c. Baltimore's ball, first and 10 from Chicago's 30.
  d. Baltimore's ball, first and 10 from the 50.

15. Improvisational drama

The Green Bay Packers are in a punting situation (fourth and 10) at their own 30-yard line. The Packers' center snaps the ball to the punter, but the punt is partially blocked by a Bears linebacker. The ball goes two yards beyond the line of scrimmage to the Packers' 32, where it touches one of the Packers' players. It then rebounds behind the line of scrimmage, and the punter picks it up at his 25. He then throws a pass to his wide receiver, who catches it at the Packers' 35 and runs 65 yards, into the Bears' end zone. The fans at Lambeau Field go crazy. Cool-headed as ever, how do you rule it?

    a. Touchdown for Green Bay.
    b. Green Bay's ball, first and 10 from its 25.
    c. Chicago's ball, first and 10 from Green Bay's 25.
    d. Chicago's ball, first and 10 from Green Bay's 32.

16. Changing roles in mid-career

With fourth down and goal to go at Cincinnati's 2-yard line, Cleveland lines up for a field goal attempt. The holder kneels at the Bengals' 9, with the kicker ready to move forward. The snap from center is high, and the ball goes off the holder's hands. It rolls to Cincinnati's 12, where the kicker picks it up and throws a legal forward pass to his tight end, who catches it at the line of scrimmage and runs into the end zone. What do you rule?

a. Touchdown for Cleveland.
b. Touchback.
c. Cincinnati's ball, first and 10 from its 9.
d. Cincinnati's ball, first and 10 from its 12.

17. Meanwhile, in another part of our nation's capital . . .

St. Louis has the ball on the Washington 45-yard line, third down and 15. The Cardinals' quarterback fakes a pass and hands the ball to his running back on a draw play. The back runs to the Redskins' 30, where he fumbles and a Redskin recovers. During the running back's progress, a Washington defensive back holds a St. Louis wide receiver at the Redskins' 40. How do you rule it?

a. Redskins' ball, first and 10 at their own 15 (after a 15-yard penalty from where the ball was recovered).

b. Cardinals' ball, first and 10 at the Redskins' 40 (after a five-yard penalty for defensive holding, measured from the spot of the previous snap).

c. Cardinals' ball, first and 10 at the Redskins' 35 (after a five-yard penalty for defensive holding from the spot of the foul).

d. Cardinals' ball, first and 10 at the Redskins' 15 (after a 15-yard penalty against the Redskins, measured from the spot of the fumble and the ball's being returned to the Cardinals).

18. Funny, he was here just a minute ago

Cleveland faces second down and 10 on Houston's 40-yard line. A Cleveland running back goes downfield, close to the sideline, trying to get open for a pass. A Houston linebacker legally chucks him out of bounds. The running back immediately comes back onto the field of play and jumps to try to catch a perfectly thrown pass. With the ball in the air, the linebacker pushes the running back again, but the latter makes the catch anyway. He runs the ball into Houston's end zone. How do you rule it?

a. Touchdown for Cleveland.
b. Cleveland's ball, second and 10 at Houston's 40.
c. Cleveland's ball, third and 10 at Houston's 40.
d. Cleveland's ball, third and 25 at its 45.

19. Something extra times two

New Orleans has the ball on its own 40-yard line. It is third down and 10. A New Orleans running back is tackled at his 36, where he fumbles, then bats the loose ball forward from his 36 to his 42. There, a New Orleans teammate recovers the ball. New Orleans was offside. How do you rule it?

a. New Orleans's ball, third and 29 on its 21.
b. New Orleans's ball, fourth and 8 from its 42.
c. New Orleans's ball, third and 15 from its 35.
d. New Orleans's ball, third and 25 from its 25 (after a 15-yard penalty from the spot of the previous snap).

20. Volleying deep

San Diego has third down and 18 from its 4-yard line. The Chargers' quarterback throws a forward pass from his end zone. The ball is batted back by a Houston linebacker. It goes right back into the quarterback's hands. He is standing in the end zone. He then flips the ball forward to one of his running backs, who also is in the end zone. The running back is tackled immediately. He fumbles. The Houston linebacker who originally batted the ball now recovers it in the end zone. How do you rule it?

   a. San Diego's ball, fourth and 18 on its 4.
   b. San Diego's ball, fourth and 20 on its 2.
   c. Touchdown for Houston.
   d. Safety against San Diego.

21. Worth putting in the playbook?

The Los Angeles Rams' kicker attempts a field goal from the San Francisco 30-yard line, seven yards behind the line of scrimmage. The kick is wide. The ball touches a 49er as he tries to catch it in the end zone. It then rolls out to the 49ers' 3, where the Rams' tight end falls on it. What would you rule?

a. Rams' ball, first down at the 49ers' 30.
b. Touchback.
c. 49ers' ball, first and 10 from their 23.
d. 49ers' ball, first and 10 from their 30.

22. The ultimate dump-off

On third and 15 from his 4-yard line, the Baltimore quarterback takes the snap from his center and drops back into the end zone to throw a forward pass. A Cincinnati defensive end crashes through and is about to tackle the quarterback, when he intentionally throws the ball down in front of himself while in the end zone. The defensive end falls on the ball in the end zone. How would you rule it?

    a. Safety.
    b. Touchdown.
    c. Colts' ball, fourth and 15 from their 4.
    d. Colts' ball, fourth and 17 from their 2.

23. Please hold all applause

On third down with the ball on Miami's 8-yard line, New England's quarterback takes the snap. He immediately throws a backward pass to his fullback, who can't quite catch the ball. The fullback juggles it as he is running forward, and the ball falls out of his hands on the 5-yard line. The fullback never had control of it. The ball rolls into Miami's end zone, where a Miami safety picks it up and runs the length of the field, into New England's end zone. How would you rule it?

a. Touchdown.
b. Touchback.
c. Safety.
d. Incomplete pass, fourth down for New England on Miami's 8-yard line.

24. Catch!

Washington's return man waits for a punt in his own end zone. He comes out of the end zone, catches the ball a foot or so in front of the goal line, and steps back into the end zone. He then flips the ball to the field judge covering the play. The field judge blows his whistle. What is the correct call?

  a. Touchback.
  b. Safety.
  c. Inadvertent whistle. Put the ball in play on the Washington 1-yard line.
  d. Re-play the entire play.

25. Don't look back

On fourth down, with the ball at New Orleans's 40-yard line, the Saints' punter stands with his hands outstretched, waiting to receive the snap from center. The ball sails over the punter's head and lands on the Saints' 20. The punter, meanwhile, has turned and is trying to recover the ball. However, a San Francisco defensive end pushes the punter from behind, moving him out of the way. The 49ers' defender then picks up the ball on New Orleans's 15-yard line and runs it into the Saints' end zone. How would you rule it?

- a. Touchdown.
- b. Clipping penalty against San Francisco, 15 yards from the spot of the snap. First down for New Orleans.
- c. 49ers' ball, first down where the defensive end recovered the ball (the 15).
- d. 49ers' ball, first down with a 15-yard penalty against the 49ers from the spot where the pushing took place.

26. Transition game

Denver kicks off to start the game. The Houston return man waits in his end zone. He tries to catch the ball there, but it slips through his hands. He bends over to pick up the ball in the end zone and accidentally kicks it out to his 10-yard line. A Denver player picks it up and runs it into Houston's end zone. Before he has crossed the goal line, one of his teammates holds a Houston player at the 6. How would you rule it?

a. Touchdown for Denver and a 15-yard penalty against Houston on the ensuing kickoff.
b. Denver's ball, first down on the Houston 10.
c. Denver's ball, first down on the Houston 21.
d. Safety against Houston for kicking a loose ball in its end zone.

27. Letting go

It is Denver's ball, second down and 20 from its 30. The Broncos' quarterback drops back and throws a forward pass. Just as the ball leaves his hand, a blitzing Dallas linebacker roughs the quarterback. Denver's wide receiver catches the ball at midfield and runs to the Dallas 40, where he is tackled and fumbles. Dallas recovers the ball on its own 35. How would you rule it?

a. Denver's ball, first down at its 45, after penalizing Dallas 15 yards from the spot of the previous snap.

b. Denver's ball, first down at Dallas's 40.

c. Denver's ball, first down at Dallas's 25, after penalizing Dallas 15 yards from the spot of the fumble.

d. Dallas's ball, first down from its 15-yard line, after penalizing the Cowboys 15 yards from where they recovered.

28. Coming to grips

Minnesota faces second down on Baltimore's 40-yard line. The Vikings' quarterback drops back to pass. One of the Colts' defensive tackles comes in from the "blind side" and tackles the quarterback, who drops the ball before he hits the ground. A Colts player picks up the ball at midfield and runs it into the Vikings' end zone. While the quarterback was dropping back to pass, a Colts linebacker held a Vikings wide receiver on the Colts' 30-yard line. How would you rule it?

a. Touchdown, holding penalty against Baltimore on the ensuing kickoff.
b. Minnesota's ball, first down on the Colts' 25.
c. Minnesota's ball, first down on the Colts' 30.
d. Minnesota's ball, first down on the Colts' 35.

29. Homemade option play

St. Louis has the ball, fourth down and two yards to go at Pittsburgh's 8-yard line. St. Louis lines up for a field goal. The snap is high and goes off the hands of the holder, who is kneeling at Pittsburgh's 15. The kicker picks up the ball and tries to run for a first down or a touchdown. He runs to Pittsburgh's 7 and spots an eligible receiver in the end zone. He throws the ball from the 7. One of the Pittsburgh defenders pushes the eligible receiver from behind as he tries to catch the ball. The ball hits the goal post, and the receiver catches it in the end zone before it hits the ground. What would you rule?

   a. Touchback for Pittsburgh.
   b. St. Louis's ball, first down on Pittsburgh's 1-yard line.
   c. Touchdown for St. Louis.
   d. Pittsburgh's ball, first down on its 12.

30. The opposite of "Captain, may I?"

Minnesota faces second down on Los Angeles's 20-yard line. The Vikings' quarterback throws a pass to his wide receiver, but a Rams' defensive back intercepts on his 2-yard line, with his back to his own goal line. The backward momentum carries him one step, then a second step, backward. He is just inside the goal line when he is tackled and downed. How would you rule it?

   a. Safety against the Rams.
   b. Touchback for the Rams, first down on their 20.
   c. Rams' ball, first down on their 2.
   d. Rams' ball, first down on their 1.

NFL Lists

If you're a fan of cubbyholes and compartments, you'll probably wonder why we've omitted categories such as "left-footed outside linebackers of the NFC East." Our apologies. And while we're cross-referencing our archives for more related irrelevance, you'll have to satisfy yourself with the groups that appear here. It goes without saying that each sub-heading is quiz bait in itself. So why did we say it?

1. What they REALLY do for a living

Off-field occupations of some NFL players:

Tom Pridemore, Falcons .... West Virginia State Legislator
Allan Ellis, Bears .... Male model
Lenny Walterscheid, Bears .. U.S. Ski Patrol member
Butch Johnson, Cowboys .... Jazz disc jockey
Aaron Kyle, Cowboys ...... Advertising copy writer
Elmer Collett, Colts .... Gold prospector
David Hill, Lions .... Television cameraman
Nick Bebout, Seahawks ..... Stock car driver
Ray Brown, Saints .... Novelist
Neil Olkewicz .... Deputy sheriff

2. Ten times the number from Olive Branch, Mississippi

Ten NFL players from Shreveport, Louisiana:
1. Terry Bradshaw, Steelers
2. Joe Ferguson, Bills
3. Isaac Hagins, Buccaneers
4. Jim Harlan, Redskins
5. Bo Harris, Bengals
6. Ezra Johnson, Packers
7. Gary Johnson, Chargers
8. Tom Owen, Patriots
9. Robert Pennywell, Falcons
10. Charles Philyaw, Raiders

3. Next of kin

Brothers who have played in the NFL:

1. Ted, Lou, and Alex Karras
2. Bill, Rich, and Ron Saul
3. Phil and Merlin Olsen
4. Ed and Dick Modzelewski
5. Tody and Bubba Smith
6. Marvin and Gene Upshaw
7. Art and Benny Malone
8. Steve and Nick Mike-Mayer
9. Bob and Dick Anderson
10. Dewey and Lee Roy Selmon
11. Chuck Muncie and Nelson Munsey
12. Lyle and Glenn Blackwood

4. Lead oxen

All-Time Top 10 Rushers:

PLAYER	YEARS	ATT.	YARDS	AVG.	LONG	TD
Jim Brown	9	2,359	12,312	5.2	80	106
O.J. Simpson	11	2,404	11,236	4.7	94	61
Jim Taylor	10	1,941	8,597	4.4	84	83
Franco Harris	8	2,012	8,563	4.3	75	72
Joe Perry	14	1,737	8,378	4.8	78	53
Larry Csonka	11	1,891	8,081	4.3	54	64
Leroy Kelly	10	1,727	7,274	4.2	70	74
Walter Payton	5	1,548	6,926	4.5	76	59
John Riggins	9	1,666	6,822	4.1	66	42
John Henry Johnson	13	1,571	6,803	4.3	87	48

Tommy Prothro, director of player personnel for the Cleveland Browns, was hit on the head by a foul ball while watching a baseball game at Portland's Multnomah Stadium. The batter at the time was his father, "Doc" Prothro, who played major league ball with the Washington Senators, Boston Red Sox, and Cincinnati Reds and later managed the Philadelphia Phillies.

5. On the wing

All-time Top 10 Passers*:

PLAYER	YEARS	ATT.	COMP.	PCT. COMP.	YARDS	TD	RATING
Roger Staubach	11	2,958	1,685	57.0	22,700	153	83.5
Sonny Jurgensen	18	4,262	2,433	57.1	32,224	255	82.8
Len Dawson	19	3,741	2,136	57.1	29,711	239	82.6
Fran Tarkenton	18	6,467	3,686	57.0	47,003	342	80.5
Bert Jones	7	1,592	890	55.9	11,435	78	80.3
Bart Starr	16	3,149	1,808	57.4	24,718	152	80.3
Ken Stabler	10	2,481	1,486	59.9	19,078	150	79.9
Ken Anderson	9	2,785	1,570	56.4	20,030	125	79.1
Johnny Unitas	18	5,186	2,830	54.6	40,239	290	78.2
Otto Graham	6	1,565	872	55.7	13,499	88	78.1

*To qualify for the list, a player must have made 1,500 or more attempts. The passing ratings are based on performance standards established for completion percentage, interception percentage, touchdown percentage, and average gain. Passers are allocated points according to how their marks compare with those standards.

6. Highly receptive

All-Time Top 10 Pass Receivers:

PLAYER	YRS.	NO.	YDS.	AVG.	LONG	TD
Charley Taylor	13	649	9,110	14.0	88	79
Don Maynard	15	633	11,834	18.7	87	88
Raymond Berry	13	631	9,275	14.7	70	68
Fred Biletnikoff	14	589	8,974	15.2	82	76
Lionel Taylor	10	567	7,195	12.7	80	45
Lance Alworth	11	542	10,266	18.9	85	85
Bobby Mitchell	11	521	7,954	15.3	99	65
Billy Howton	12	503	8,459	16.8	90	61
Harold Jackson	12	497	8,840	17.8	79	70
Tommy McDonald	12	495	8,410	17.0	91	84

7. Prolific

All-Time Top 10 Scorers:

PLAYER	YEARS	TD	FG	PAT	TP
George Blanda	26	9	335	943	2,002
Jim Turner	16	1	304	521	1,439
Jim Bakken	17	0	282	534	1,380
Fred Cox	15	0	282	519	1,365
Lou Groza	17	1	234	641	1,349
Jan Stenerud	13	0	279	394	1,231
Gino Cappelletti*	11	42	176	350	1,130
Bruce Gossett	11	0	219	374	1,031
Don Cockroft	12	0	200	393	993
Garo Yepremian	12	0	192	407	983

*Cappelletti's total includes four two-point conversions.

8. Familiar with paydirt

All-Time Top 10 Touchdown Scorers:

PLAYERS	YEARS	RUSH	PASS REC.	RETURNS	TOTAL TD
Jim Brown	9	106	20	0	126
Lenny Moore	12	63	48	2	113
Don Hutson	11	3	99	3	105
Jim Taylor	10	83	10	0	93
Bobby Mitchell	11	18	65	8	91
Leroy Kelly	10	74	13	3	90
Charley Taylor	13	11	79	0	90
Don Maynard	15	0	88	0	88
Lance Alworth	11	2	85	0	87
Paul Warfield	13	0	85	1	86

Compton (California) Junior College listed the following former NFL players as coaches of its 1978 football team: head coach Art Perkins and assistants Marlin Briscoe, Henry Dyer, Essex Johnson, Deacon Jones, and Joe Sweet. Also stopping by, on occasion, were Lawrence McCutcheon and Ron Jessie of the Los Angeles Rams. Compton's record in 1978 was 3–7.

9. Paragons of patience

Nineteen men who played all ten seasons of the American Football League, 1960–69:

1. George Blanda
2. Billy Cannon
3. Gino Cappelletti
4. Larry Grantham
5. Wayne Hawkins
6. Jim (Earthquake) Hunt
7. Harry Jacobs
8. Jack Kemp
9. Paul Lowe
10. Jacky Lee
11. Bill Mathis
12. Paul Maguire
13. Don Maynard
14. Ron Mix
15. Jim Otto
16. Babe Parilli
17. Johnny Robinson
18. Paul Rochester
19. Ernie Wright

10. Time capsule

All-AFL Team:

Offense	Defense
Fred Arbanas, TE	Jerry Mays, DE
Ron Mix, T	Tom Sestak, DT
Billy Shaw, G	Houston Antwine, DT
Jim Otto, C	Gerry Philbin, DE
Ed Budde, G	George Webster, LB
Jim Tyrer, T	Nick Buoniconti, LB
Lance Alworth, WR	Bobby Bell, LB
Don Maynard, WR	Willie Brown, CB
Joe Namath, QB	Dave Grayson, CB
Paul Lowe, RB	Johnny Robinson, S
Clem Daniels, RB	George Saimes, S
George Blanda, K	Jerrel Wilson, P

11. So what became of 33?

Number 32 was considered the number of prominent running backs (e.g., Jim Brown, O.J. Simpson, Franco Harris) for many years. Today's stars wear number 34:

Earl Campbell, Oilers
Tony Galbreath, Saints
Terdell Middleton, Packers
Walter Payton, Bears
Greg Pruitt, Browns
Rickey Young, Vikings

12. The "farm system"

Top 10 colleges sending players into the NFL*:

1. USC   37
2. Oklahoma   31
3. Colorado   29
4. Penn State   26
5. UCLA   25
6. Ohio State   24
7. Nebraska   21
8. San Diego State 21
9. Notre Dame   19
10. Alabama   18

In 1960, the offensive backfield for Taft High School in Cincinnati was Al Nelson, quarterback, and Walter Johnson, Carl Ward, and Cid Edwards, running backs. Nelson played safety for the Philadelphia Eagles (1965–1973); Johnson played defensive tackle for the Cleveland Browns (1965–1976); Ward was a safety with Cleveland (1967–68) and New Orleans (1969); and Edwards was a running back with St. Louis (1968–1971), San Diego (1972–74), and Chicago (1975).

*From 1980 veteran rosters

13. Indoor-outdoor specialists

Ten NFL players who also played professional basketball:

Player, NFL Team	Basketball Team and First Year
1. Bud Grant, Eagles	Minneapolis Lakers, 1950–51
2. Connie Mack Berry, Bears	Oshkosh All-Stars, 1940–41
3. Otto Graham, Browns	Rochester Royals, 1946–47
4. Dick Evans, Packers	Sheboygan Redskins, 1941–42
5. Ted Fritsch, Packers	Oshkosh All-Stars, 1945–46
6. Len Ford, Browns	Dayton Rens, 1949–50
7. Otto Schnellbacher, Giants	St. Louis Bombers, 1948–49
8. Bob Shaw, Rams	Youngstown Bears, 1945–46
9. Ron Widby, Cowboys	New Orleans Buccaneers, 1967–68
10. Lonnie Wright, Broncos	Denver Rockets, 1967–68

14. How long does it take?

For an NFL team to complete summer training camp .... 45 days
To complete an NFL game .... 3 hours
For an NFL team to complete a practice session .... 1½ hours
For a wide receiver to cover 40 yards .... 4.4 seconds
For a 250 pound lineman to cover 40 yards. 5.1 seconds
For a good punt to stay in the air (hang time) .... 5.0 seconds
To convert an NFL stadium from baseball to football .... 8 hours
For a quarterback to drop back and set up to pass .... 2.3 seconds
For the average NFL player to complete his career .... 4.3 years

15. NFL Olympians

PLAYER	YEAR	EVENT	MEDAL
1. Jim Thorpe	1912	decathlon,	gold
		pentathlon	gold
2. Harold (Brick) Muller	1920	high jump	silver
3. Jim Bausch	1932	decathlon	gold
4. Pete Mehringer	1932	wrestling (light heavyweight)	gold
5. Jack Torrance	1936	shot put	none
6. Ollie Matson	1952	400 meters, 1,600 meter relay	bronze, gold

7. Milt Campbell	1952,	decathlon	silver,
	1956	decathlon	gold
8. Colin Ridgway	1956	high jump	none
9. Glenn Davis	1956,	intermediate hurdles,	gold
	1960	intermediate hurdles	gold
		1,600 meter relay	gold
10. Bo Roberson	1960	long jump	silver
11. Ray Norton	1960	100 meters,	none,
		200 meters,	none,
		400 meter relay	gold
12. Frank Budd	1960	100 meters	none
13. Henry Carr	1964	200 meters,	gold
		1,600 meter relay	gold,
14. Bob Hayes	1964	100 meters,	gold
		400 meter relay	gold,
15. Jim Hines	1968	100 meters,	gold
		400 meter relay	gold
16. Tommie Smith	1968	200 meters	gold
17. Larry Burton	1972	200 meters	none
18. Gerald Tinker	1972	400 meter relay	gold
19. James Owens	1976	110 meter high hurdles	none

16. Fixtures

Top 11 active players with most games played:

1. Jim Turner, K, Broncos 228
2. Paul Krause, S, Vikings 226
3. Wally Hilgenberg, LB, Vikings 199
4. Alan Page, DT, Bears 186
5. Jan Stenerud, K, Chiefs 186
6. Gene Upshaw, G, Raiders 186
7. Randy Rasmussen, G, Jets 184
8. Ken Houston, S, Redskins 183
9. Bob Matheson, LB, Dolphins 180
10. Larry Little, G, Dolphins 178
11. Craig Morton, QB, Broncos 178

When the NFL and the All-America Football Conference merged for the 1950 season, a showdown game between Philadelphia and Cleveland was scheduled on the Saturday night before the regular Sunday opening for the rest of the league. The Eagles were two-time champions of the NFL. The Browns had won the AAFC title all four years of that league's existence. The Browns won the game 35–10, but Eagles coach Earle (Greasy) Neale was quoted as calling the Browns "a basketball team that can only pass." In the return match on December 3, 1950, the Browns did not throw a single pass. They beat the Eagles 13–7.

17. Still churning

Top 10 Active Rushers:

	YEARS	ATTEMPTS	YARDS	TD
1. Franco Harris, Pittsburgh	8	2012	8563	72
2. Larry Csonka, Miami	11	1891	8081	64
3. Walter Payton, Chicago	5	1548	6926	59
4. John Riggins, Washington	9	1666	6822	42
5. Lydell Mitchell, San Diego	8	1668	6518	30
6. Lawrence McCutcheon, Denver	8	1435	6186	23
7. Calvin Hill, Cleveland	10	1447	6049	42
8. Chuck Foreman, New England	7	1533	5887	52
9. Greg Pruitt, Cleveland	7	1087	5255	25
10. Sam Cunningham, New England	7	1290	5163	39

18. Pitch till you win

Top 10 Active Passers:

	ATT.	COMP.	PCT. COMP.	YARDS	TD	RATE PTS.
1. Bert Jones, Baltimore	1592	890	55.9	11,435	78	80.3
2. Ken Stabler, Houston	2481	1486	59.9	19,078	150	79.9
3. Ken Anderson, Cincinnati	2785	1570	56.4	20,030	125	79.1
4. Bob Griese, Miami	3329	1865	56.0	24,302	186	77.0
5. Greg Landry, Baltimore	2204	1227	55.7	15,383	95	73.6
6. Dan Fouts, San Diego	2005	1141	56.9	14,739	82	73.0
7. Pat Haden, Los Angeles	1055	574	54.4	7,296	43	72.8
8. Brian Sipe, Cleveland	1637	902	55.1	11,075	77	71.9
9. Bill Munson, Buffalo	1982	1070	54.0	12,896	84	71.6
10. Craig Morton, Denver	3083	1627	52.8	22,370	150	71.4

19. Good hands people

Top 10 Active Pass Receivers:

	YEARS	NO.	YARDS	TD
1. Harold Jackson, New England	12	497	8840	70
2. Harold Carmichael, Philadelphia	9	407	6080	57
3. Bob Tucker, Minnesota	10	407	5248	26
4. Haven Moses, Denver	12	395	7171	51
5. Ken Burrough, Houston	10	377	6343	42
6. Lydell Mitchell, San Diego	8	374	3182	17
7. Reggie Rucker, Cleveland	10	368	5765	39
8. Charlie Joiner, San Diego	11	354	6156	36
9. Ahmad Rashad, Minnesota	7	345	4619	32
10. Chuck Foreman, New England	7	336	3057	23

20. Mostly just for kicks

Top 10 Active Scorers:

	YEARS	TD	FG	PAT	TP
1. Jim Turner, Denver	16	1	304	521	1439
2. Jan Stenerud, Kansas City	13	0	279	394	1231
3. Don Cockroft, Cleveland	12	0	200	393	993
4. Garo Yepremian, New Orleans	12	0	192	407	983
5. Mark Moseley, Washington	9	0	152	235	691
6. Toni Fritsch, Houston	8	0	119	221	578
7. Chester Marcol, Green Bay	8	0	118	148	502
8. Franco Harris, Pittsburgh	8	76	0	0	456
9. Chuck Foreman, New England	7	75	0	0	450
10. John Smith, New England	6	0	79	202	439

The AFL adopted the two-point conversion option for its first season of play in 1960. The point value was two if successfully converted by a pass or running play, one if kicked in the conventional manner.

21. Not just a nickname

In 1922 and 1923, Marion, Ohio, had an NFL franchise that was sponsored by the Oorang Airedale Kennels. The team, known as the Oorang Indians and coached by Jim Thorpe, was made up of native Americans. A partial list of the players:

1. Arowhead
2. Black Bear
3. Deerslayer
4. Xavier Downwind
5. Laughing Gas
6. Joe Little Twig
7. Red Fang
8. Stilwell Sanooke
9. Baptiste Thunder
10. Wrinkle Meat
11. Deadeye
12. Lone Wolf

22. Papa Bear says

George Halas's list of the twelve best quarterbacks he's seen:

1. Sid Luckman: " 'Mr. Quarterback' . . . the first of the modern quarterbacks . . . set the pattern for man-in-motion T-formation."
2. Sammy Baugh: "Fired a bullet-like pass with the flick of his wrist . . . tremendous player to watch . . . poised at all times."
3. Otto Graham: "Team leader, unflinching when the going got tough . . . knew how to make a play work."
4. Bobby Layne: "Fiery, skilled quarterback . . . great field general . . . dominant figure on the field, team leader."
5. Bart Starr: "Cool and calculating . . . tremendous respect from teammates . . . a fine field general with a great arm."
6. Fran Tarkenton: "The first scrambling quarterback . . . his records speak for his durability and talent."
7. Johnny Unitas: "Great poise and leadership . . . a pressure player with full confidence of team . . . outstanding passer with great knowledge of the game."
8. Norm Van Brocklin: "Highly emotional, skilled leader . . . strong arm, great timing on long or short passes."
9. Bob Waterfield: "Superb, confident quarterback . . . versatile as runner, passer, punter, placekicker, and defender . . . inspiring leader."
10. Terry Bradshaw: "An outstanding field general . . . strong and accurate passer . . . great physical equipment . . . a winner."
11. Roger Staubach: "Inspirational leader . . . very cool in pressure situations . . . dangerous from anywhere, at anytime."
12. Ken Stabler: "Outstanding late in the game, when points are needed . . . thrives in clutch situations."

23. Now look, Dean . . . .

The nine current NFL officials who are ex-NFL players:

1. Ron Botchan, Chargers, Oilers
2. Royal Cathcart, 49ers
3. Pat Harder, Cardinals, Lions
4. Pat Knight, Giants
5. Dean Look, Jets
6. Leo Miles, Giants
7. Lou Palazzi, Giants
8. Frank Sinkovitz, Steelers
9. Fred Wyant, Redskins

24. Nice going, junior

Five NFL players who won the Heisman Trophy as college juniors:

1. Doak Walker, Southern Methodist, 1948—Lions
2. Vic Janowicz, Ohio State, 1950—Redskins
3. Roger Staubach, Navy, 1963—Cowboys
4. Archie Griffin, Ohio State, 1974—Bengals
5. Billy Sims, Oklahoma, 1978—Lions

Former NFL Commissioner Bert Bell, under whose direction the League reached new stability and acceptance, suffered a fatal heart attack while attending the Philadelphia Eagles-Pittsburgh Steelers game at Franklin Field, October 11, 1959. Bell had been associated with both teams as a coach and executive prior to taking over as Commissioner in 1946.

25. Laugh all you want . . .

Twelve men who have played in the NFL:

1. June Jones
2. Margene Adkins
3. Gail Cogdill
4. Blenda Gay
5. Fair Hooker
6. Dolly King
7. Blanche Martin
8. Kay McFarland
9. Julie Rykovich
10. Bev Wallace
11. Faye Wilson
12. Tillie Manton

26. And they're all close friends of Howard Cosell

Ivy Leaguers in the NFL:

1. Dick Jauron, Bengals, Yale
2. Pat McInally, Bengals, Harvard
3. Reggie Williams, Bengals, Dartmouth
4. Calvin Hill, Browns, Yale
5. Carl Barisich, Dolphins, Princeton
6. John Spagnola, Eagles, Yale
7. Tim Mazzetti, Falcons, Pennsylvania
8. Dan Jiggetts, Bears, Harvard
9. Gary Fencik, Bears, Yale
10. Karl Chandler, Lions, Princeton
11. George Starke, Redskins, Columbia

27. Where have you gone, Haywood Sullivan?

Major league baseball players drafted by the NFL:

	PLAYER	COLLEGE	NFL TEAM	ROUND	YR.
1.	Sam Chapman	California	Redskins	2	1938
2.	George (Snuffy) Stirnweiss	N. Carolina	Chicago Cardinals	2	1940
3.	Alvin Dark	LSU	Eagles	2	1945
4.	Walt Dropo	Connecticut	Bears	9	1946
5.	Lloyd Merriman	Stanford	Chicago Cardinals	3	1947
6.	Bill Renna	Santa Clara	Rams	12	1949
7.	Haywood Sullivan	Florida	Chicago Cardinals	25	1953
8.	Norm Cash	Sul Ross State	Bears	13	1955
9.	Jake Gibbs	Mississippi	Browns	9	1961
10.	Merv Rettenmund	Ball State	Cowboys	19	1965
11.	Dave Winfield	Minnesota	Vikings	17	1973

28. Global

Eight foreign-born NFL players:

1. Rick Berns, RB, Buccaneers—Okinawa
2. Jack Thompson, QB, Bengals—American Samoa
3. Frank Manumaleuga, LB, Chiefs—Laie, Samoa
4. Mosi Tatupu, RB, Patriots—Pago Pago, Samoa
5. Ted Hendricks, LB, Raiders—Guatemala City, Guatemala
6. Art Kuehn, C, Seahawks—Victoria, British Columbia, Canada
7. Tony Daykin, LB, Falcons—Taipei, Taiwan
8. David Whitehurst, QB, Packers—Baumholder, Germany

For a brief time during the offseason in 1950 the NFL was known as the "National-American Football League." This was after the merger of the NFL and the All-America Football Conference, which saw the Baltimore Colts, Cleveland Browns, and San Francisco 49ers join the established league from the defunct AAFC.

29. Coming at it from a different angle

Foreign-born kickers in the NFL:

1. Neil O'Donoghue, Buccaneers—Dublin, Ireland
2. Nick Mike-Mayer, Bills—Bologna, Italy
3. Steve Mike-Mayer, Colts—Budapest, Hungary
4. Jan Stenerud, Chiefs—Fetsund, Norway
5. Garo Yepremian, Saints—Laruala, Cyprus
6. Uwe von Schamann, Dolphins—West Berlin, Germany
7. John Smith, Patriots—Leafield, England
8. Rafael Septien, Cowboys—Mexico City, Mexico
9. Benny Ricardo, Lions—Asuncion, Paraguay
10. Chester Marcol, Packers—Opole, Poland
11. Frank Corral, Rams—Chihuahua, Mexico

30. Blocks and their respective chips

Twelve NFL father/son combinations:

1. Tony and Mike Adamle
2. Harold and Hal Bradley
3. Jim and Walker Gillette
4. John and Jack Gregory
5. Herb and John and Charley Hannah
6. Dub and Bert Jones
7. George and Jim Kiick
8. Bill and Pete Lazetich
9. Gil and Jim Stienke
10. Wilford (Whizzer) and Danny White
11. Ray and Mike Renfro
12. Elwyn and Bill Dunstan

31. Versatile

Ten players from other sports drafted by the NFL:

PLAYER	COLLEGE	N.F.L. TEAM	ROUND	YR.	SPORT
1. Mel Patton	USC	Giants	21	1946	track
2. K. C. Jones	San Francisco	Rams	30	1955	basketball
3. Johnny Kerr	Illinois	49ers	26	1955	basketball
4. Dave Sime	Duke	Lions	29	1959	track
5. Randy Matson	Texas A&M	Falcons	5	1967	track
6. Dave Lattin	Texas Western	Chiefs	17	1967	basketball
7. Jimmy Walker	Providence	Saints	17	1967	basketball
8. Joe Cowan	Johns Hopkins	Colts	12	1969	lacrosse
9. Willie Davenport	Southern U.	Saints	12	1970	track
10. Bart Buetow	Minnesota	Vikings	3	1972	hockey

32. Back to haunt them

Ten quarterbacks who won championships after being traded or waived:

1. George Blanda, from Chicago Bears to Houston Oilers
2. Len Dawson, Cleveland Browns to Kansas City Chiefs
3. Jack Kemp, San Diego Chargers to Buffalo Bills
4. Bobby Layne, New York Bulldogs to Detroit Lions
5. Earl Morrall, New York Giants to Baltimore Colts
6. Bill Nelsen, Pittsburgh Steelers to Cleveland Browns
7. Frank Ryan, Los Angeles Rams to Cleveland Browns
8. Fran Tarkenton, New York Giants to Minnesota Vikings
9. Y.A. Tittle, San Francisco 49ers to New York Giants
10. Norm Van Brocklin, Los Angeles Rams to Philadelphia Eagles

The last NFL team to switch to the T-formation was the Pittsburgh Steelers. After clinging to the single-wing years longer than the other teams, they made the changeover for the 1952 season.

33. Very carefully

How NFL teams call their plays:

American Conference

Team	How the play is called
Baltimore	Quarterback
Buffalo	Messenger/wide receivers
Cincinnati	Messenger/tight ends
Cleveland	Quarterback
Denver	Messenger/wide receivers
Houston	Quarterback
Kansas City	Quarterback
Miami	Quarterback
New England	Messenger/wide receivers
New York Jets	Quarterback
Oakland	Quarterback
Pittsburgh	Quarterback
San Diego	Messenger/wide receivers
Seattle	Messenger/wide receiver-tight ends

National Conference

Team	How the play is called
Atlanta	Messenger/wide receivers
Chicago	Quarterback
Dallas	Messenger/tackles-guards
Detroit	Quarterback
Green Bay	Hand signals
Los Angeles	Hand signals
Minnesota	Quarterback
New Orleans	Quarterback
New York Giants	Hand signals
Philadelphia	Hand signals
St. Louis	Quarterback
San Francisco	Quarterback
Tampa Bay	Hand signals
Washington	Hand signals

34. The University of Coaching

Sixteen NFL coaches from Miami University (Ohio):

1. Paul Brown — Bengals and Browns
2. Weeb Ewbank — Browns, Colts, and Jets
3. Howard Brinker — Browns and Bengals
4. John Brickels — Browns
5. Sid Gilman — Rams, Chargers, Oilers, Bears, and Eagles
6. Fritz Heisler — Browns
7. John McVay — Giants and 49ers
8. Bruce Beatty — Patriots and Lions
9. Clive Rush — Jets and Patriots
10. Doc Urich — Broncos, Bills, and Redskins
11. Bill Arnsparger — Dolphins, Colts, and Giants
12. Ken Meyer — Jets, Rams, 49ers, and Bears
13. Jack Faulkner — Rams, Broncos, Saints, Vikings, and Chargers
14. Ed Biles — Saints, Jets, and Oilers
15. Jerry Wampfler — Eagles, Bills, and Giants
16. Joe Galat — Giants

The relatively small Oxford, Ohio, school has sent Woody Hayes, Ara Parseghian, Colonel Earl (Red) Blaik, Bo Schembechler, John Pont, Paul Dietzel, Carmen Cozza, Bill Mallory, and Dick Crum to the college coaching ranks. Former Dodger manager Walt Alston also is a Miami man.

35. Not-so-ancient history

Cities that have had NFL franchises:

CITY	TEAM	FIRST YEAR IN NFL
1. Canton, Ohio	Bulldogs	1920
2. Columbus, Ohio	Panhandles	1920
3. Dayton, Ohio	Triangles	1920
4. Duluth, Minnesota	Eskimos	1926
5. Evansville, Indiana	Crimson Giants	1922
6. Hammond, Indiana	Pros	1920
7. Hartford, Connecticut	Blues	1926
8. Portsmouth, Ohio	Spartans	1930
9. Pottsville, Pennsylvania	Maroons	1925
10. Providence, Rhode Island	Steamrollers	1925
11. Racine, Wisconsin	Legions	1922
12. Rochester, New York	Jeffersons	1920

36. Not a prerequisite

Current NFL coaches who did and did not play in the NFL:

Did	Did Not
Mike McCormack, Colts	Chuck Knox, Bills
Forrest Gregg, Bengals	Sam Rutigliano, Browns
Don Shula, Dolphins	Red Miller, Broncos
Walt Michaels, Jets	Bum Phillips, Oilers
Tom Flores, Raiders	Marv Levy, Chiefs
Chuck Noll, Steelers	Ron Erhardt, Patriots
Jack Patera, Seahawks	Don Coryell, Chargers
Neill Armstrong, Bears	Leeman Bennett, Falcons
Tom Landry, Cowboys	Ray Malavasi, Rams
Monte Clark, Lions	Dick Vermeil, Eagles
Bud Grant, Vikings	Jim Hanifan, Cardinals
Dick Nolan, Saints	Bill Walsh, 49ers
Ray Perkins, Giants	John McKay, Buccaneers
Jack Pardee, Redskins	
Bart Starr, Packers	

Playing like the archetypal "Paper Lions," the Detroit Lions went winless (0–11) in 1942, giving up 263 points while scoring only 38.

37. As an actor, he's a helluva football player

Some NFL players who have acted in motion pictures:

1. Sammy Baugh.......King of the Texas Rangers
2. Jim Boeke...................North Dallas Forty
3. Ben Davidson.......................M*A*S*H
4. Brian Duncan.....................Semi-Tough
5. Carl Eller.......................The Black Six
6. Fred Gehrke......................Easy Living
7. Frank Gifford................Darby's Rangers
8. Red Grange................One Minute to Play
9. Joe Greene...............Pop Goes the Weasel
10. Tom Harmon.............Harmon of Michigan
11. Mike Henry.......................Tarzan '65
12. Elroy Hirsch.......................Crazylegs
13. Mike Lucci........................Paper Lion
14. Bruce Smith..............Smith of Minnesota
15. Bob Waterfield..................Triple Threat

38. What does it MEAN?

In 10 of 14 Super Bowls, the winning quarterback has worn number 12:

Game III—Joe Namath, New York Jets
Game VI—Roger Staubach, Dallas Cowboys
Game VII—Bob Griese, Miami Dolphins
Game VIII—Bob Griese, Miami Dolphins
Game IX—Terry Bradshaw, Pittsburgh Steelers
Game X—Terry Bradshaw, Pittsburgh Steelers
Game XI—Ken Stabler, Oakland Raiders
Game XII—Roger Staubach, Dallas Cowboys
Game XIII—Terry Bradshaw, Pittsburgh Steelers
Game XIV—Terry Bradshaw, Pittsburgh Steelers

39. Centurions

NFL head coaches who have won 100 or more games:

COACH	TEAM(S)	YRS.	WON	LOST	TIED
George Halas	Chicago Bears	40	320	147	30
Earl (Curly) Lambeau	Green Bay Packers, Chicago Cardinals, Washington Redskins	33	231	133	23
Tom Landry	Dallas Cowboys	20	172	104	6
Don Shula	Baltimore Colts, Miami Dolphins	17	175	62	5
Paul Brown	Cleveland Browns, Cincinnati Bengals	21	166	100	6
Steve Owen	New York Giants	23	151	100	17
Hank Stram	Kansas City Chiefs, New Orleans Saints	17	131	97	10
Weeb Ewbank	Baltimore Colts, New York Jets	20	130	129	7
Bud Grant	Minnesota Vikings	12	122	59	5
Sid Gillman	Los Angeles Rams, San Diego Chargers, Houston Oilers,	18	122	99	7
George Allen	Los Angeles Rams, Washington Redskins	12	116	47	5
Raymond (Buddy) Parker	Chicago Cardinals, Detroit Lions, Pittsburgh Steelers	15	104	75	9
John Madden	Oakland Raiders	10	103	32	7
Chuck Noll	Pittsburgh Steelers	11	100	57	1

REGULAR SEASON

40. You can't get there from here

TEAM	TRAINING CAMP LOCATION
Atlanta Falcons	Suwanee, Georgia
Baltimore Colts	Towson, Maryland
Buffalo Bills	Niagara, New York
Chicago Bears	Lake Forest, Illinois
Cincinnati Bengals	Wilmington, Ohio
Cleveland Browns	Kent, Ohio
Dallas Cowboys	Thousand Oaks, California
Denver Broncos	Fort Collins, Colorado
Detroit Lions	Rochester, Michigan
Green Bay Packers	DePere, Wisconsin
Houston Oilers	San Angelo, Texas
Kansas City Chiefs	Liberty, Missouri
Los Angeles Rams	Fullerton, California
Miami Dolphins	Miami, Florida
Minnesota Vikings	Mankato, Minnesota
New England Patriots	Smithfield, Rhode Island
New Orleans Saints	Vero Beach, Florida
New York Giants	Pleasantville, New York
New York Jets	Hempstead, New York
Oakland Raiders	Santa Rosa, California
Philadelphia Eagles	West Chester, Pennsylvania
Pittsburgh Steelers	Latrobe, Pennsylvania
St. Louis Cardinals	St. Charles, Missouri
San Diego Chargers	La Jolla, California
San Francisco 49ers	Santa Clara, California
Seattle Seahawks	Cheney, Washington
Tampa Bay Buccaneers	Tampa, Florida
Washington Redskins	Carlisle, Pennsylvania

The 1963 Minnesota Vikings hold the NFL record for the most fumbles recovered in a season, 58. Of that number, Vikings recovered 27 of their own fumbles while taking possession of 31 opponents' mistakes. Individual honors, if that's the correct term for fumbles lost, go to Oakland quarterback Dan Pastorini. In 1973, while playing with Houston, he committed 17 fumbles—an NFL record.

41. Be it ever so humble . . .

TEAM	STADIUM AND CAPACITY	YEAR OPENED
Atlanta Falcons	Atlanta-Fulton County Stadium (60,498)	1965
Baltimore Colts	Memorial Stadium (60,020)	1954
Buffalo Bills	Rich Stadium (80,020)	1973
Chicago Bears	Soldier Field (58,064)	1926
Cincinnati Bengals	Riverfront Stadium (59,754)	1970
Cleveland Browns	Cleveland Stadium (80,385)	1932
Dallas Cowboys	Texas Stadium (65,101)	1971
Denver Broncos	Denver Mile High Stadium (75,103)	1948
Detroit Lions	Pontiac Silverdome (80,638)	1975
Green Bay Packers	Lambeau Field (56,194) and Milwaukee County Stadium (55,958)	1957
Houston Oilers	Astrodome (50,000)	1953
Kansas City Chiefs	Arrowhead (78,094)	1965
Los Angeles Rams	Anaheim Stadium (69,000)	1972
Miami Dolphins	Orange Bowl (75,250)	1966
Minnesota Vikings	Metropolitan Stadium (48,446)	1938
New England Patriots	Schaefer Stadium (61,297)	1956
		1971

NFL playing sites:

Team	Stadium	Year
New Orleans Saints	Louisiana Superdome (71,330)	1975
New York Giants	Giants Stadium (76,500)	1976
New York Jets	Shea Stadium (60,372)	1964
Oakland Raiders	Oakland-Alameda County Coliseum (54,615)	1966
Philadelphia Eagles	Philadelphia Veterans Stadium (71,434)	1971
Pittsburgh Steelers	Three Rivers Stadium (54,000)	1970
St. Louis Cardinals	Busch Memorial Stadium (51,392)	1966
San Diego Chargers	San Diego Stadium (52,660)	1967
San Francisco 49ers	Candlestick Park (61,185)	1960
Seattle Seahawks	Kingdome (64,757)	1976
Tampa Bay Buccaneers	Tampa Stadium (72,112)	1967
Washington Redskins	Robert F. Kennedy Stadium (50,045)	1961

42. There's more than one way

Thirteen members of the Pro Football Hall of Fame who didn't play in the NFL:

1. Bert Bell .... Commissioner
2. Charles Bidwill, Sr. .... Owner
3. Paul Brown .... Coach
4. Joe Carr .... League President
5. Weeb Ewbank .... Coach
6. Lamar Hunt .... Founder, Owner
7. Vince Lombardi .... Coach
8. George Preston Marshall .... Owner
9. Tim Mara .... Owner
10. Earle (Greasy) Neale .... Coach
11. Hugh (Shorty) Ray ...... Supervisor of Officials
12. Dan Reeves .... Owner
13. Art Rooney, Sr. .... Owner

43. Take me out to the ballgame

Six former NFL teams:

TEAM	YEAR
1. Cleveland Indians	1921 and 1923
2. New York Yankees	1927-28
3. Brooklyn Dodgers	1930-1943
4. Boston Braves	1932
5. Pittsburgh Pirates	1933-39
6. Texas Rangers*	1952

* When the franchise was awarded, the team was known as the Texas Rangers, but the name was changed to the Dallas Texans before the start of the 1952 season (two other NFL teams with major league baseball counterparts are the New York Giants and the St. Louis Cardinals).

44. Sometimes not even a bridesmaid

Seven NFL teams that have never won a league or world championship:

1. Atlanta Falcons
2. Cincinnati Bengals
3. New England Patriots
4. New Orleans Saints
5. San Francisco 49ers
6. Seattle Seahawks
7. Tampa Bay Buccaneers

Two former NFL players have served in the U.S. House of Representatives. Lavern Dilweg, an end with the Milwaukee Badgers (1926) and the Green Bay Packers (1927–1934), ran as a Democrat in Wisconsin and was elected for a single term, 1940–42. Jack Kemp, a former quarterback with the Pittsburgh Steelers (1957), Los Angeles Chargers (1960), San Diego Chargers (1961–62), and Buffalo Bills (1962–69), now serves as a Republican from New York State.

45. Big Apple big time

Professional football franchises in New York City:

TEAM AND LEAGUE	YEAR
New York Giants (NFL)	1925-present
Brooklyn Horsemen (AFL)	1926
Brooklyn Lions (NFL)	1926
New York Yankees (AFL)	1926
New York Yankees (NFL)	1927-28
Stapleton Stapes (NFL)	1929-32
Brooklyn Dodgers (NFL)	1930-43
Brooklyn Tigers (AFL)	1936
New York Yankees (AFL)	1936
New York Yankees (AFL)	1940
New York Americans (AFL)	1941
Brooklyn Tigers (NFL)	1944
Brooklyn Dodgers (AAFC)	1946-48
New York Yankees (AAFC)	1946-48
Brooklyn-N.Y. Yankees (AAFC)	1949
New York Bulldogs (NFL)	1949
New York Yanks (NFL)	1950-51
New York (Titans) Jets (NFL-AFL)	1960-present
New York Stars (WFL)	1974

46. The big ones that got away

Six quarterbacks who were (briefly) Pittsburgh Steelers:

1. Len Dawson
2. Jack Kemp
3. Sid Luckman
4. Earl Morrall
5. Bill Nelson
6. Johnny Unitas

47. O.K., but just for a year or two

Ten Houston Oilers head coaches in the team's 20-year history:

COACH	YEARS	RECORD
Lou Rymkus	1960-61	11-7-1̂
Wally Lemm	1961	9-0-0
Frank (Pop) Ivy	1962-63	17-11-0
Sammy Baugh	1964	4-10-0
Hugh (Bones) Taylor	1965	4-10-0
Wally Lemm	1966-70	28-38-4
Ed Hughes	1971	4-9-1
Bill Peterson	1972-73	1-18-0
Sid Gillman	1973-74	8-15-0
O.A. (Bum) Phillips	1975-79	43-29-0

48. Wire to wire

Longest plays:
   Kickoff return: 106 yards, Roy Green, St. Louis vs. Dallas, 1979; Noland Smith, Kansas City vs. Denver, 1967; Al Carmichael, Green Bay vs. Chicago Bears, 1956.
   Fumble return: 104 yards, Jack Tatum, Oakland vs. Green Bay, 1972.
   Interception return: 102 yards, Gary Barbaro, Kansas City vs. Seattle, 1977; Erich Barnes, New York Giants vs. Dallas, 1961; Bob Smith, Detroit vs. Chicago Bears, 1949.
   Pass play: 99 yards, Sonny Jurgensen to Gerry Allen, Washington vs. Chicago, 1968; Karl Sweetan to Pat Studstill, Detroit vs. Baltimore, 1966; George Izo to Bobby Mitchell, Washington vs. Cleveland, 1963; Frankie Filchock to Andy Farkas, Washington vs. Pittsburgh, 1939.
   Punt return: 98 yards, Dennis Morgan, Dallas vs. St. Louis, 1974; Charlie West, Minnesota vs. Washington, 1968; Gil LeFebvre, Cincinnati vs. Brooklyn, 1933.
   Run from scrimmage: 97 yards, Bobby Gage, Pittsburgh vs. Chicago Bears, 1949; Andy Uram, Green Bay vs. Chicago Cardinals, 1939.

49. Jock in the booth

Twelve former NFL players who are now sportscasters:

1. Tom Brookshier
2. John Brodie
3. Irv Cross
4. Len Dawson
5. Frank Gifford
6. Paul Hornung
7. Don Meredith
8. Johnny Morris
9. Merlin Olsen
10. Roger Staubach
11. Pat Summerall
12. Fran Tarkenton

50. Hold that (chorus) line

NFL teams with cheerleading groups:

Atlanta Falcons	Cheerleaders
Baltimore Colts	Cheerleaders
Buffalo Bills	Jills
Chicago Bears	Honey Bears
Cincinnati Bengals	Ben-gals
Dallas Cowboys	Cheerleaders
Green Bay Packers	The Sideliners
Houston Oilers	Derrick Dolls
Kansas City Chiefs	Chiefettes
Los Angeles Rams	Cheerleaders
Miami Dolphins	Starbrites
Minnesota Vikings	Parkettes
New England Patriots	Spirits of New England
Oakland Raiders	Raiderettes
Philadelphia Eagles	Liberty Belles
St. Louis Cardinals	Big Red Line
Seattle Seahawks	Sea-gals
Tampa Bay Buccaneers	Swash-buc-lers
Washington Redskins	Redskinettes

Answers

Answers to "NFL Trivia Quiz"

1. d
2. b
3. e
4. b
5. b
6. b
7. c. Bezdek managed the Pittsburgh Pirates in 1917, 1918, and 1919 and coached the Cleveland Rams in 1937 and 1938.
8. a. Merlin Olsen, b. Alan Page, c. Joe Greene, d. Manny Fernandez, e. Ed (Too Tall) Jones.
9. False. Willie Wood is not an enshrinee, but Herb Adderley is.
10. Joe (The Jet) Perry played for Compton J.C. Dick (Night Train) Lane played for Scottsbluff J.C.
11. f
12. c
13. a. Curley Culp was an NCAA heavyweight wrestling champion at Arizona State.
14. d. Hank Soar played for the New York Giants (1937–44 and 1946), umpired in the American League (1950–71), and coached the Providence Steamrollers in the BAA, a forerunner to the NBA (1947–48).
15. c
16. b
17. d
18. b. Smith, a quarterback from Alabama, played with the Redskins from 1936–38. Jay Berwanger, the first overall choice in the draft, elected not to play.
19. a
20. a
21. e
22. b

23. c
24. b
25. 1-i, 2-e, 3-h, 4-c, 5-j, 6-f, 7-g, 8-k, 9-a, 10-m, 11-l, 12-d, 13-b.
26. a
27. b
28. They all played quarterback in the NFL after playing college football for Don Coryell at San Diego State. In addition, two of Coryell's former quarterbacks are NFL assistants. Wayne Sevier is special teams coach on Coryell's Chargers' staff. Rod Dowhower is offensive coordinator of the Denver Broncos.
29. b
30. c
31. d
32. e
33. c
34. c
35. c
36. Los Angeles Rams, Detroit Lions, Chicago Bears, Baltimore Colts, Cincinnati Bengals, Denver Broncos, and Miami Dolphins.
37. b
38. False. The only teams to do it were the Philadelphia Eagles of 1948 and 1949. They shut out the Chicago Cardinals 7–0 in 1948 and the Los Angeles Rams 14–0 in 1949.
39. d
40. c
41. a. Ewbank coached the 1958 and 1959 Baltimore Colts and the 1968 New York Jets to world titles.
42. b
43. d
44. False. Billy (White Shoes) Johnson of the Houston Oilers is the leader with 13.4 yards.
45. False. Gillom's 43.8 yard average ranks fourth on

166

the all-time list behind Sammy Baugh's **45.1,** Tommy Davis's 44.7, and Yale Lary's 44.3.
46. b. Albert played with the 49ers from 1946–1952.
47. True
48. a
49. False. Foreman led the NFC in scoring and receiving but finished second by six yards to Jim Otis of the Cardinals in rushing.
50. Offense: 1-f, 2-d, 3-b, 4-k, 5-h, 6-c, 7-a, 8-j, 9-g, 10-e, 11-i.
    Defense: 1-h, 2-c, 3-d, 4-g, 5-a, 6-i, 7-k, 8-j, 9-f, 10-e, 11-b.
51. Elmer Layden. Jim Thorpe, Joe Carr, and Carl Storck all held the title of President. The other three Horsemen were quarterback Harry Stuhldreher, halfback Jim Crowley, and fullback Don Miller.
52. b
53. True
54. Big Ten: 1-j, 2-h, 3-b, 4-a, 5-d, 6-c, 7-f, 8-e, 9-g, 10-i;
    Pac-10: 1-j, 2-i, 3-h, 4-g, 5-e, 6-f, 7-c, 8-d, 9-b, 10-a;
    Big Eight: 1-b, 2-c, 3-d, 4-f, 5-a, 6-g, 7-e, 8-h;
    Southwestern Conference: 1-c, 2-d, 3-e, 4-g, 5-f, 6-i, 7-h, 8-b, 9-a;
    Southeastern Conference: 1-b, 2-d, 3-f, 4-i, 5-a, 6-h, 7-e, 8-j, 9-c, 10-g;
    Independents: 1-d, 2-j, 3-a, 4-h, 5-c, 6-e, 7-g, 8-i, 9-f, 10-b.
55. b
56. Brooklyn Dodgers, Buffalo Bisons, Chicago Rockets, Cleveland Browns, Los Angeles Dons, Miami Seahawks, New York Yankees, and San Francisco 49ers.
57. b
58. False. Gale Sayers, with a 30.6 average, is the all-time leader.

59. a
60. True
61. a
62. d
63. b. The move was made in 1937.
64. f. Both Gent (a wide receiver from Michigan State) and Green (a cornerback from Utah State) had played basketball in college.
65. False. There are seven: referee, umpire, head linesman, line judge, field judge, back judge, and side judge.
66. e
67. c
68. c. Gehrke is now vice-president and general manager of the Denver Broncos.
69. f
70. False. Minnesota's Paul Krause moved ahead of Tunnell in 1979. Krause's total is 81, Tunnell's 79.
71. e
72. e
73. d
74. d
75. d. Gary McDermott, a second-year running back, was already wearing number 32, but he gave up the number in time for Simpson to wear it in the first regular season game of 1969.
76. e
77. e
78. c
79. b
80. f. The Redskins won the game.
81. True
82. b
83. False. The Youngbloods are not even related. Ron (Redskins) and Rich Saul (Rams) are the NFL's only twins.
84. d

85. True. The other AFL's existed in 1926, 1936–37, and 1940–41.
86. a
87. 1-g, 2-d, 3-c, 4-h, 5-j, 6-a, 7-e, 8-i, 9-f, 10-b.
88. St. Louis Cardinals, Philadelphia Eagles, Seattle Seahawks, and Atlanta Falcons.
89. c
90. f. Simpson gained 2,003 yards in 1973.
91. c. Blanda, playing for Houston, threw for 36 touchdowns in 1961. He was intercepted 42 times in 1962.
92. b. The Packers have won 11 league titles: 1929, 1930, 1931, 1936, 1939, 1944, 1961, 1962, 1965, 1966, and 1967.
93. e. Campbell gained 1,697 yards.
94. c. The Browns set the record during their 42–21 victory over the Chicago Bears in 1951.
95. d. Dempsey's kick was 63 yards.
96. f. The Tampa Bay Buccaneers lost the first 26 games they ever played; all 14 in 1976 and the first 12 of 1977.
97. c. In 1975 Metcalf gained 2,462 yards in the following categories: rushing, 816 yards; receiving, 378; punt returns, 285; kickoff returns, 960. He also advanced a fumble 23 yards.
98. d. Thrower played for the Chicago Bears in 1953.
99. b. Contrary to trivia legend, Y.A. Tittle was not a third member of the LSU backfield at that time.
100. f. As youngsters, the brother and sister were playing and Jeanne told Erny of a vision she had of his becoming a famous football player. He was an All-American at USC and played with the Boston/Washington Redskins, 1932–40.
101. f. Carson admits to being hooked on such soaps as "The Edge of Night," "As the World Turns," and "The Secret Storm" since childhood.
102. a. DeBerg's 578 attempts and 347 completions sur-

passed Tarkenton's 572 and 345 (established in 1978).

103. c. Brown led the NFL in eight of the nine seasons he played.

104. f. Moore scored in the final two games of the 1963 season, all 14 games of 1964, and the first two of 1965.

105. c. As an expansion team the Cowboys could not participate in the NFL draft. They signed Perkins (a halfback from New Mexico) and Meredith (a quarterback from Southern Methodist) to personal services contracts and acquired their rights (Perkins from the Baltimore Colts and Meredith from the Chicago Bears).

106. f. Grupp averaged 43.6 yards on 89 punts. His net average of 37.2 led the league in that category.

107. e. Harder, who played with the Chicago Cardinals (1946–1950), and the Detroit Lions (1951–53) made nine PATs against the New York Giants in 1948. He is in his fifteenth season as an NFL official.

108. b

109. c. Hultz, a defensive tackle, made nine recoveries with the Minnesota Vikings in 1963.

110. d. The 49ers attempted 602 passes and completed 361 for 3,760 yards.

111. a. Sam Cunningham gained 768 yards, Horace Ivory 693, Andy Johnson 675, and Steve Grogan 539.

112. False. Although the Super Bowl was televised by two networks, the networks were NBC, which did the AFL regular season games, and CBS, which showed the NFL regular season.

113. e. Fred Williamson referred to his karate-like forearm chop as "the hammer" and speculated that he might just wipe out the entire Packers' offense.

114. c

115. b

116. False. The Pittsburgh Steelers won their first Super Bowl appearance, game IX.
117. c
118. False. Joe Kapp was the quarterback when the Vikings lost Super Bowl IV to the Kansas City Chiefs.
119. c
120. a. The controversy arose over whether or not Renfro touched the ball. If he didn't—and he maintained he did not—it would have been illegal under then-existing rules for two members of the offensive team (Hinton and Mackey) to touch the ball without a member of the defense touching it.
121. b
122. d. Alworth spent most of his career with the Chargers; Ditka with the Bears and Eagles.
123. d
124. b
125. False. Larry Cole, Cliff Harris, D.D. Lewis, Preston Pearson, Charlie Waters, and Rayfield Wright also have played in five Super Bowls.
126. d. The 17 net yards yielded by the Steelers defense still stands as a Super Bowl record.
127. a
128. b
129. False. Although Pearson has played in five Super Bowls, he's done it with only three teams—Colts, Steelers, and Cowboys.
130. True
131. c. Brown's return is a Super Bowl record.
132. True
133. b
134. c
135. True. The Cowboys had won VI and XII, the Steelers IX and X.
136. True. Cole started at left defensive end in Super Bowl V, right defensive tackle in game X, and left defensive tackle in game XIII.

137. True
138. c. Starr I and II, Namath III, Dawson IV, Staubach VI, and Bradshaw XIII and XIV.
139. d. Dallas linebacker Chuck Howley (the only player from a losing team so honored) won the award in Super Bowl V.
140. d. Harris won the award in Super Bowl IX, Csonka in VIII.
141. False. Safety Jake Scott, Miami Dolphins, was presented with the award for Super Bowl VII.
142. False. Swann won in Super Bowl X, Fred Biletnikoff of the Raiders won in Super Bowl XI, and Stallworth has not won the award.
143. d. It was the Minnesota Vikings' rallying cry for Super Bowl IV.
144. b
145. True. Dwight White in Super Bowl IX, and Reggie Harrison in Super Bowl X.
146. False. Tom Landry's two Super Bowl victories were in VI and XII.
147. False. Don Shula took the Colts and the Dolphins to the Super Bowl.
148. False. The leading interceptor is *linebacker* Chuck Howley of the Dallas Cowboys. He picked off three in two games.
149. False. Landry has lost three of the five games the Cowboys have played, but Bud Grant has lost all four of the Minnesota Vikings' Super Bowl games.
150. False. Super Bowl VIII was played in Rice Stadium, Houston, Texas.

Answers to "You Make the Call"

1. d. The fumble was in the end zone. When a foul occurs during a fumble, as it did on this play, enforcement of the foul is from the spot of the fumble. If the offense (in this case, San Diego) commits a

foul *anywhere,* and the spot of enforcement is behind its goal line, it is ruled a safety.

2. b. If a member of the offensive team lifts a runner to his feet, it is ruled illegal use of hands. The penalty is 15 yards from the spot of the foul.

3. c. It is a foul if a player pushes an opponent, unless it is in a legal *personal* attempt to recover a loose ball. On this play, a Detroit player pushed an opponent, not in a personal attempt to recover the ball but to enable a teammate to recover it. This is ruled a defensive foul for illegal use of hands. The penalty is five yards. It is enforced from the spot of the previous snap (4-yard line). Any defensive foul behind the spot of the previous snap is enforced from that spot (i.e., in this case, the 4).

4. b. The kicker kicked a loose ball, which is a foul. The ball went over the end line after it crossed the crossbar. This is ruled a touchback, as the kicking team has put the ball out of its opponents' end zone. Had the kicker been able to gain full possession of the ball, he would have been permitted to drop-kick it, for example.

5. b. It was a safety. The ball is ruled dead when it hits the shaft of the goal marker, which is considered out-of-bounds. Therefore, Dallas fell on a dead ball in the end zone, which had no bearing on the play. Washington had possession of the ball last, before it went out-of-bounds. On a fumble out-of-bounds, possession goes to the team that last controlled the ball. In this case, the ball was declared out-of-bounds, and Washington had put the ball into its own end zone, thereby creating a safety. The offensive clip (by Washington), as the ball was rolling loose, further confused the issue. The kickoff following the safety should be from the Redskins' 10-yard line rather than from its 20, as is customary following a safety. On a scoring play, when a personal foul occurs and

the foul didn't contribute to the score, the penalty is assessed on the next kickoff. A clip is a personal foul.

6. c. This was an illegal forward pass, as it was thrown from beyond the line of scrimmage. The penalty for the foul is loss of down and five yards from the spot of the illegal pass.

7. c. This is considered a free kick (kickoff) out of bounds. When the Atlanta player recovered the ball with one foot on the sideline, the play was dead. The last player to have touched the ball before it went out of bounds was a Falcon. If a member of the kicking team (offensive team) is the last player to have touched the ball before it goes out of bounds, it is ruled a re-kick with a five-yard penalty. If the defensive team is the last one to touch the kickoff ball before it goes out of bounds, the ball is awarded to the defensive team at the spot where it goes out.

8. c. This is considered an illegal forward pass thrown from beyond the line of scrimmage. This type of pass calls for a five-yard penalty from the spot of the pass and a loss of down. However, Minnesota made more than enough for the first down, and after the ball was placed on the 10-yard line, the Vikings still had their first down. When the forward pass (though illegal) hit the ground, the ball was dead, and no further action could take place on that ball. Therefore, Detroit recovered a dead ball, so the Lions couldn't take possession legally.

9. d. The Minnesota player who threw the ball down in his own end zone was actually throwing a backward pass. If a backward pass hits the ground, the ball is not dead. In this case, the ball rolled out to the 2-yard line, where the Bears recovered. That's legal, but a backward pass that hits the ground can not be advanced by the defensive team if they recover it. In this situation, the ball is dead where it is recovered. A backward pass is defined as any pass that is not a forward pass. A forward pass is one that moves

toward the opponent's goal line. The pass on this play was toward the Minnesota player's own goal line and therefore was a backward pass.

10. c. This is considered a foul during a running play. The foul occurred on the 2-yard line. The NFC is awarded possession and a first down on the AFC's 1-yard line (half the distance to the goal). The spot of enforcement for a foul on a running play, if the foul occurs at the end of the run, is the spot of the foul. If the NFC player merely had fumbled and there had been no foul, it would have been a touchback.

11. d. The move was an illegal forward pass, as the ball was handed forward on a play that was not begun at scrimmage. The penalty is five yards from the spot of the pass (forward handoff, in this case). The ball is dead when handed forward and possessed by the second ball handler. If the second Ram had *dropped* the ball after the handoff, it also would have been ruled a dead ball.

12. a. A player may use his hands in a personal legal attempt to recover a loose ball. If the Ram had pushed the Raider out of the way to enable one of his teammates to recover the ball, it would have been illegal use of hands. The ball then would return to Oakland with a first down. However, this play is legal all the way.

13. b. It is a touchdown, not pass interference. Pass interference rules do not apply to an illegal pass unless it is a second pass from behind the line of scrimmage. This was an illegal pass, as the passer threw the ball from beyond scrimmage. Illegal passes may be intercepted.

14. b. The ball must touch the ground beyond the receiving team's restraining line, which in this case was Chicago's 45-yard line, or be touched by a member of the receiving team, in order for either side to take possession.

15. d. No player of the kicking team may touch a scrimmage kick before it has been touched by a receiver. If an illegal touch occurs, it is ruled the receivers' ball at the spot of illegal touching, which in this case was Green Bay's 32. Though the punt was partially blocked, it remained a kicked ball because it crossed the line of scrimmage and was not touched by a Chicago player beyond that point. A Green Bay player was the first to touch the kicked ball beyond the line of scrimmage, thus it became Chicago's ball at the spot of the illegal touch, the 32.

16. d. This was a fourth down fumble play. Cleveland's holder was the player considered to have fumbled the ball. The fourth down fumble rule states that if a fourth down fumble occurs and the recovery is by another offensive player, the spot of the next snap is the spot of the fumble, unless the spot of recovery is behind the spot of the fumble, in which case it becomes the spot of recovery. Cleveland's holder was not eligible to recover the ball, as no defensive player touched it after the holder fumbled on Cincinnati's 9. The Browns' kicker picked up the ball behind the spot of the fumble, so the ball is dead there. Cleveland didn't make the necessary yardage for a first down, so Cincinnati takes over on its 12-yard line.

17. c. This was a foul on a running play with a change of possession (from Cardinals to Redskins). If a foul occurs during a running play (which this was, because the Cardinals' ball carrier ran from scrimmage), and the run on which the foul occurs is followed by a change of possession, the spot of enforcement is the spot of the foul. The foul (defensive holding) took place at the Redskins' 40-yard line, and the penalty for that foul is five yards.

18. c. If a legal receiver goes out of bounds accidentally or is forced out by a defender, and he (the receiver) returns to touch or catch a pass inbounds, the play is treated as a pass touched or caught out of bounds.

No penalty yardage is involved. No pass interference is called on an action involving an ineligible receiver, which was what the Cleveland running back became when he went out of bounds, so the Houston linebacker's shove was nothing. The pass should be ruled incomplete.

19. b. The defensive team would logically refuse both the illegal bat and the offside, making the situation fourth down. New Orleans would then have to punt, giving up the ball. If the defensive team were to accept either penalty, the situation would be third down again. That would give New Orleans an opportunity to try for a first down.

20. a. The Chargers' quarterback threw a second forward pass from behind the line of scrimmage. The ruling is loss of down, and the ball is placed at the spot of the previous snap. A second forward pass is an illegal pass. In this case, when it was caught, the play was over. The subsequent fumble recovery didn't count.

21. c. A missed field goal from outside the 20-yard line returns to the spot where it was snapped. If the ball had touched a 49er in the field of play, and then the Rams' tight end had fallen on it, it would have been the Rams' ball there.

22. d. This was intentional grounding of a forward pass. The penalty is 15 yards and a loss of down. Because the play started from the 4-yard line, the penalty goes to the 2 (half the distance to the goal, in this case) with a loss of down.

23. b. Because the fullback never had possession of the backward pass, it remained a backward pass. No defensive player may advance a backward pass if he recovers the ball after it touches the ground. The ball is dead where it is recovered. Because the fullback was the person responsible for putting the ball into Miami's end zone and it was recovered there by Miami, it is a touchback. The ball is put in play by Miami with a first down at its 20.

24. b. The return man put the ball into his own end zone after having caught it in the field of play.

25. c. This is considered a backward pass, not a fumble. A backward pass may be advanced by the defense only if the ball is caught in flight. No defensive player may advance a backward pass if he recovers the ball after it touches the ground. In that case, the ball is dead where it is recovered. The recovering team takes over at the spot of recovery. It is legal for a player to push an opponent out of the way and to use his hands in an actual attempt to recover a loose ball.

26. b. Though kicking a loose ball is a violation, it is penalized from the kickoff spot, because it still is a kick. Denver would naturally refuse the penalty to keep the ball. The Broncos can only recover the ball, not advance it, because Houston never had possessed it. The penalty against Denver for holding would be ignored because it took place during a dead ball and therefore wasn't a personal foul. The ball became dead when it was recovered by the kicking team.

27. c. When a team commits a personal foul (e.g., roughing the passer) prior to the completion of a legal forward pass from behind the line of scrimmage, the offended team benefits from a 15-yard penalty enforced from the spot where the ball is dead beyond the line of scrimmage. The exception to the rule is that if the offended team (Denver) loses possession after a completion, enforcement is from where possession was lost (in this case, the Cowboys' 40-yard line), and the ball reverts to the offended team.

28. d. This was defensive holding against the Colts on a running play. When the spot of enforcement is behind the line of scrimmage, as was the case here, any penalty yardage is assessed from the spot of the previous snap. A defensive holding penalty is five yards. This was not pass interference because the ball never was thrown.

29. d. St. Louis threw an illegal pass. The passer went

bevond the line of scrimmage and threw from the 7.
There is no defensive pass interference on an illegal
pass. The ball became dead when it hit the goal post,
so the St. Louis receiver caught a dead ball. The penalty against St. Louis for a pass thrown from behind
the line of scrimmage is loss of down and five yards
from the spot of the pass. The ball was thrown from
the 7-yard line on fourth down. It then became Pittsburgh's ball, first down on the Steelers' 12.

30. b. Both of the defensive back's feet would have had
to touch in the field of play for "intercepting momentum" to have been ruled. The player's second step
took him and the ball into the end zone. Had his second foot touched in the field of play, and had he carried the ball (due to "intercepting momentum") into
the end zone, the ball would have gone back to where
he intercepted it (the Rams' 2).

ABOUT THE AUTHORS

Ted Brock, 37, was born in Los Angeles and grew up in the San Francisco Bay area, where his appreciation of football was enriched by an incurable sentimentality about the University of California Bears and the San Francisco 49ers. Before joining NFL Properties, Inc. as an associate editor in 1977, he worked as a high school English teacher and a freelance sports writer.

Jim Campbell, 43, is a native of Pennsylvania. He and Brock have co-authored "NFL Trivia" for *PRO!*, the official magazine of the NFL, for three seasons. A graduate of Susquehanna University, Campbell has been on the staff of NFL Properties, Inc. since 1977. Prior to that he was an historian at the Pro Football Hall of Fame in Canton, Ohio.

SIGNET Books You'll Enjoy

☐ **HOW TO KNOW THE BIRDS by Roger Tory Peterson.** Here is an authoritative, on-the-spot guide to help you recognize instantly most American birds on sight. Includes a 24-page color supplement. (#J9278—$1.95)

☐ **HOW TO KNOW THE AMERICAN MARINE SHELLS by R. Tucker Abbott.** Revised edition. A definitive guide to the shells of our Atlantic and Pacific coasts—featuring a digest of shell-fishery laws, a list of shells by location, full-color photographs, and black and white drawings. (#W6528—$1.50)

☐ **THE HAMMOND ALMANAC OF A MILLION FACTS, RECORDS, FORECASTS, 1981.** For home, school, and office—the most comprehensive and up-to-date one-volume encyclopedia for quick and easy reference. Twelfth annual edition, with full-color and black and white maps, important tax tips, how to trace your family's roots, and more! (#XE2061—$4.95)

☐ **GOUSHA-CHEK-CHART NORTH AMERICAN ROAD ATLAS.** The most informative, up-to-date atlas on the market today. Features individual maps of all 50 states plus Canada and Mexico, with city indexes and legends right on each state and province; a full color relief map of North America; and distance charts listed in both miles and kilometers. (#XE2064—$4.50)

☐ **COLLECTING STAMPS by Paul Villard.** Everything you need to know to pursue one of the world's most popular hobbies for fun, knowledge, and profit. (#J6522—$1.95)

Buy them at your local

bookstore or use coupon

on next page for ordering.

More MENTOR and SIGNET Reference Books

☐ **ALL ABOUT WORDS by Maxwell Numberg and Morris Rosenblum.** Two language experts call on history, folklore, and anecdotes to explain the origin, development, and meaning of words. (#ME1879—$2.25)

☐ **HOW DOES IT WORK? by Richard Koff.** A practical and entertaining guide to the workings of everyday things—from air conditioners to zippers. Illustrated. (#W6920—$1.50)

☐ **BEGIN CHESS by D. B. Pritchard.** An introduction to the game and to the basics of tactics and strategy. Foreword by Samuel Reshevsky, International Grand Master and former American chess champion. (#W9516—$1.50)

☐ **WORDS OF SCIENCE and the History Behind Them by Isaac Asimov.** A famous author makes the language of science accessible to all. Some 1500 terms are traced through history, from their simple roots in the language of bygone times—to their complicated usages today. (#MJ1799—$1.95)

☐ **WORDS FROM THE MYTHS by Isaac Asimov.** A fascinating exploration of our living heritage from the ancient world. Isaac Asimov retells the ancient stories—from Chaos to the siege of Troy—and describes their influence on modern language . . . and modern life. (#W9362—$1.50)

Buy them at your local bookstore or use this convenient coupon for ordering.

THE NEW AMERICAN LIBRARY, INC.,
P.O. Box 999, Bergenfield, New Jersey 07621

Please send me the SIGNET and MENTOR BOOKS I have checked above. I am enclosing $_____(please add $1.00 to this order to cover postage and handling). Send check or money order—no cash or C.O.D.'s. Prices and numbers are subject to change without notice.

Name _____

Address _____

City _____ State _____ Zip Code _____

Allow 4-6 weeks for delivery.
This offer is subject to withdrawal without notice.

When Kids Join
THE NFL
SUPERPRO CLUB,
They Join the NFL.

There's only one NFL and there's only one fan club that's really a part of it — the new NFL SuperPro Club. Now kids ages 8 to 14 can become members of a unique club that combines all the fun, excitement, and color of pro football.

For just $6, kids receive three great NFL SuperPro Club packages a year that'll put them right at the center of NFL action.

Look at the great NFL SuperPro Club items each member will receive:

Official I.D. Card
Official Membership Certificate
NFL SuperPro Club Iron-On T-Shirt Transfer
The First Official NFL Trivia Book
NFL Team Standings Board
NFL SuperPro Club Flying Saucer
Touch Football Playing Tips Book
NFL Team Decals
Official NFL SuperPro Club Newsletters
The Great NFL Fun Book II
Official Super Bowl XVI Poster

Sign up your NFL SuperPro today!

----
clip here and mail

Here's how to join:
Fill out the coupon below and send it with a check or money order for $6 to:
NFL SuperPro Club, P. O. Box 8888, Trenton, N. J. 08650.

Name _____ Age _____

Address _____

City/State/Zip _____

Telephone _____ Favorite Team _____

Membership kits will be mailed beginning August 20, 1981.
Please allow 4–6 weeks for delivery.